Table of Contents

Introduction 05

Breakfast Recipes

- Eggs Florentine 07
- Chocolate Waffles 08
- Sweet Potato & Carrot Rostis 08
- Chocolate French Toast 09
- Cheese Bacon Flatbreads 09
- Mushroom & Rarebit Muffins 10
- Apple Pie Porridge 10
- Banana and Maple Porridge 11
- Strawberry Oat Muffins 11
- Air Fryer Full English 12
- Strawberry Souffle Omelette 13
- Pizza Waffles 14
- Potato, Cheese and Onion Waffles 15
- BLT Sandwich 16
- Pie Overnight Oats 17
- Courgette and Butter Bean Frittata 17
- Sausage Hash 18
- Breakfast Bake 19
- English Pinwheels 20
- Peanut Butter and Jelly Baked Oats 21
- Berry Toastie 21
- Rainbow Waffles 22
- Sunshine Pancakes 23
- Breakfast Wrap 24
- Overnight oats 25
- Chocolate overnight weetabix 25

Soups
- Carrot, Orange and Thyme Soup 27
- Mulligatawny Soup 28
- Pea and Ham Soupls 29
- Curried parsnip Soup 31
- Tomato Soup & Croutons 32
- Broccoli and Stilton Soup 33
- Red Pepper and Feta Soup 34
- Spinach and Rocket Soup 35
- White Onion Soup 36
- Chicken Teriyaki Noodle Soup 37
- Rice Noodle Soup 37

Salad
- Salmon Tabbouleh Salad 38
- Chicken and Ham Wraps 39
- Kale Salad 40
- Fruit Salad 41
- Chickpeas Salad 42
- Tabbouleh 42
- Steak and Feta Salad 43
- Vegetable Couscous 44
- Spinach and Chicken Meatball Salad 45
- Beetroot and Rosemary Salad 46
- Red Pesto Chicken Salad 47
- Salmon and Zingy Salad 48
- Chicken and Bacon Caesar Salad 49
- Chicken Pesto Salad 50
- Halloumi Fries Salad 51
- Greek-Style Pasta Salad 52
- Tuna Niçoise Pasta Salad 53
- Thai-Style Chicken Salad 54

Lunch & Dinner
- Beef & Onion Pasties 56
- Baked Garlic Salmon 57
- Pork Fillet 58
- Herb Crusted Cod... 59
- Salmon Spaghetti Carbonara 60
- Tricky Mac and Cheese 61
- Lemon Chicken 62

- French Dip-Style Sandwiches 63
- Bang Bang Noodles 64
- Rigatoni Pizza Pie 66
- Bacon, Onion & Potato Bake 67
- Haddock & Creamy Mustard Sauce 68
- Shepherd's Pie 69
- Creamy Mashed Potatoes 70
- Beef with Ginger & Spring Onion 71
- Garlic Mushroom Risotto 72
- Fish and Chip Pie 73
- Hunter's Chicken 74
- Cumberland Pie 75

Fakeaways

- Nando's Peri Peri Chicken 78
- Chicken Tikka Kebabs 79
- Chicken Shawarma 80
- Lamb Rogan Josh 81
- Sausage Rolls 82
- Chicken Fajitas 83
- Sesame Chicken Drumsticks 83
- Mushroom and Spinach Lasagne 84
- Chicken Jalfrezi 85
- Noodles with Chicken 86
- Chicken Korma Curry 87
- Chicken Teriyaki Kebabs 88
- Chicken Gyros Kebabs 89
- Indian-Style Fried Rice 89
- Chicken Korma Pie 90
- Tex Mex Burgers 91
- Chicken Kievs 92
- Crispy Chilli Beef 93
- Diet Coke / Pepsi Max Chicken 94
- Chicken Goujons 95
- Katsu Chicken Curry 96

Desserts & Treats

- Millionaire's Shortbread 98
- Chocolate Orange Trifles 99
- Biscoff Cheesecake 101
- Raspberry & Blueberry Baked Cheesecake 102
- Chocolate Lava Mug Cakes 103
- Chocolate Mud Pie 104
- Banana Bread with Chocolate Chips 105
- Mince Pies 105
- Apple Strudels 106
- Strawberry Souffle Omelette 107
- Peach and Blueberry Tart .... 108.
- Lemon Tiramisu 109
- Crustless Apple Pie 110
- Chocolate and Orange Cake 111
- Chocolate Brownie Trifle 112
- Biscoff Lava Cakes 113
- Banoffee Tiramisu 114
- Banana Cream Pudding 115
- Butterscotch Tarts 116
- White Chocolate Mousse with Raspberry 118
- Rice Pudding 119
- Eton Mess 119
- Christmas Trifle 120
- Christmas Chocolate Log 122
- Banana Bread Pudding 124

Introduction

There's a common misconception that healthy eating means sacrificing flavor or feeling deprived. Slimming Foodie cookbook is here to prove otherwise. Within these pages, you'll discover that nutritious, slimming-friendly meals can be just as satisfying and delicious as their higher-calorie counterparts - sometimes even more so.

Our approach is simple: we focus on whole, nutrient-dense ingredients and clever cooking techniques that maximize flavor while minimizing unnecessary calories. You won't find any "diet food" here - just real, wholesome recipes that celebrate the natural deliciousness of fresh ingredients.

What Makes These Recipes Special?

Each recipe in this collection has been carefully crafted to:

- Provide satisfying portions that keep you feeling full
- Use minimal added fats while maintaining great taste
- Incorporate plenty of vegetables and lean proteins
- Feature complex carbohydrates that provide sustained energy

Beyond the Recipes

This isn't just a collection of recipes - it's a guide to a sustainable approach to eating well. You'll find tips on meal planning, smart shopping, and cooking techniques that help you build lasting healthy habits. We've included variations for different dietary needs and preferences, proving that healthy eating can be adaptable and inclusive.

The recipes range from quick weeknight dinners to more elaborate weekend creations, showing that slimming-friendly cooking can fit any lifestyle or occasion. Whether you're cooking for yourself, your family, or entertaining friends, these dishes will prove that healthy eating never means compromising on taste or enjoyment.

Remember, this is not about restriction - it's about discovering new flavors, textures, and combinations that just happen to be good for you. Let's begin this culinary adventure together, creating meals that nourish both body and soul. Wishing you joy in the kitchen and at the table.

Emma Rogers

Breakfast

Eggs Florentine

PREP TIME 10 **COOK TIME** 20 **SERVINGS** 4

Ingredients

- 4 medium eggs
- 2 gluten free English muffins, sliced in half, approx. 60g each
- 8 g reduced fat spread, for spreading on the toasted mufins
- 200 g baby spinach leaves
- 5 g reduced fat spread, for mixing into the spinach
- small pinch of ground nutmeg
- salt and black pepper, to taste

Instructions

Make the cheese sauce: Place the milk and reduced fat spread in a medium saucepan. Place over a medium heat and stir until the spread has melted and the milk is steaming hot. Take care not to let the milk boil over.

1. Mix the cornflour and water until smooth. Mix into the hot milk, stirring constantly with a wooden spoon or balloon whisk. Bring to the boil, reduce the heat and simmer for 3-5 minutes, stirring constantly until thickened and smooth.
2. Stir in the cheese, mustard powder and season well with salt and black pepper to taste. Cover, set aside and keep warm.
3. Prepare to poach the eggs by placing a large saucepan, filled with no less than 5cm (2in) of water on the stove and bring to the boil. Reduce the heat so that the water is just simmering.
4. Meanwhile, cook the spinach. Place the spinach in a colander or sieve and rinse under cold running water. Shake well to remove the excess water and transfer the spinach to a large saucepan. Place over a low heat and cook gently, stirring constantly, for 2-3 minutes, until wilted. Take care not to overcook; the spinach should be softened but still bright green.
5. Tip the spinach into a sieve and squeeze out as much liquid as possible, using the back of a wooden spoon. Return the spinach to the saucepan and stir in the reduced fat spread, ground nutmeg and season well with salt and black pepper, to taste. Cover with a lid and keep warm.
6. To poach the eggs, gently crack the eggs into the large saucepan of simmering water, making sure they are spaced apart. Immediately lower the heat; there should only be a few small bubbles in the water. If the water is bubbling too much this may cause the eggs to move around and break up.
7. Gently poach the eggs for 2-4 minutes, depending on how you like your poached eggs to be cooked. While the eggs are poaching, toast the muffin halves until light golden and spread each with a little reduced fat spread. Place the muffin halves on four plates.
8. Divide the warm spinach between the four muffin halves, spreading out roughly over the muffins.
9. Remove the poached eggs from the cooking water using a large, slotted spoon, allowing any water to drain away. Place a poached egg on top of the spinach.
10. Pour over the warm cheese sauce and season with salt and black pepper. Serve at once.

Chocolate Waffles

PREP TIME 5　　**COOK TIME** 30　　**SERVINGS** 1

Ingredients

- 40 g oats
- 2 tsp cocoa powder
- 3/4 tbsp granulated sweetener or other sweetener to taste
- 1 tsp chocolate extract optional, but it does make it more chocolatey
- 1 medium egg
- 175 fat free natural yoghurt
- low calorie cooking spray

Instructions

1. Preheat the oven to 180°C
2. Blitz the oats in a food processor until they are quite fine and set aside
3. Add all of the ingredients to a mixing bowl and mix using a wooden spoon. Spray the waffle mould with low calorie cooking spray and pour in the mixture.
4. Bake for for 25 - 30 minutes or until the waffles are firm to the touch
5. Turn them out onto a baking tray and cook for a further 4 or 5 minutes
6. Serve with some fresh fruit and some sweetened, flavoured quark

Sweet Potato and Carrot Rostis

PREP TIME 10　　**COOK TIME** 10　　**SERVINGS** 6

Ingredients

- 2 medium sweet potatoes
- 2 medium carrots
- 1 small onion
- 2 spring onions
- 2 large eggs beaten
- 1 tsp chilli flakes
- low calorie cooking spray

Instructions

1. Grate the sweet potato and carrot into a large bowl of cold, salted water. Leave for 15 minutes to soak. Meanwhile, grate the onion and chop the spring onions.
2. Drain the potato and carrot, place into a teatowel and squeeze the excess water out. Return to the bowl and mix in the onions, spring onions and chilli flakes. Incorporate the beaten egg into the mixture and split into 6 rostis.
3. Spray a large frying pan with low calorie cooking spray and place the rostis into the pan. Leave on a low heat for at least 6 minutes - do not touch them or they will fall apart. After this time, turn quickly, in one movement and cook on the other side for 5 minutes until golden.

Chocolate French Toast

PREP TIME 5 | COOK TIME 6 | SERVINGS 1

Ingredients

- 2 thin slices wholemeal bread
- ½ tbsp chocolate hazelnut spread
- 1 small egg beaten
- ¼ tsp ground cinnamon
- 1 tsp vanilla extract
- ¼ tsp ground nutmeg
- ½ tbsp granulated sweetener
- low calorie cooking spray

Instructions

1. Mix the egg, spices, vanilla extract and sweetener in a shallow dish.
2. Cut the crusts off the bread and evenly spread the chocolate spread over one slice. Pop the second slice on top to create a sandwich.
3. Put the "sandwich" into the egg mixture. Leave to soak up the egg and spices for a minute, then turn and leave for another minute to soak on the opposite side.
4. Place a non-stick frying pan on a medium heat and spray with low calorie cooking spray. Carefully place the French Toast into the frying pan and fry on each side for about 3 minutes until golden and crisp.

Cheese Bacon Flatbreads

PREP TIME 5 | COOK TIME 7 | SERVINGS 4

Ingredients

- 4 flatbread thins folded
- 4 bacon medallions
- 80 g low fat Cheddar cheese thinly sliced
- 2 spring onions thinly sliced
- 1 tomato cut into slices
- 10 g watercress
- 2 tsp wholegrain mustard
- low calorie cooking spray

Instructions

1. Spray the griddle pan with low calorie cooking spray and place over a medium heat. Place the bacon medallions in the pan and cook for 1 - 2 minutes on each side or until cooked.
2. Unfold the flatbread and place a bacon medallion on one half of each.
3. Divide the cheese, tomato and spring onion between each and place on top of the bacon. Spread the mustard over the other half of the flatbread and fold over the filling.
4. Place on the preheated griddle pan, pressing down to produce griddle marks.
5. Cook for 3 - 5 minutes, turning occasionally, until cheese has melted. Remove from pan and carefully lift the top and add some watercress. Serve immediately.

Mushroom and Rarebit Muffins

PREP TIME 5 COOK TIME 10 SERVINGS 2

Ingredients

- 2 wholemeal English muffins
- 75 g mushrooms finely sliced
- 80 g reduced fat mature Cheddar cheese
- 1 spring onion chopped
- 1 tbsp Henderson's Relish or Worcestershire sauce
- 1 egg yolk
- 1/4 tsp mustard powder
- low calorie cooking spray
- freshly ground black pepper to taste

Instructions

1. Spray the frying pan with low calorie cooking spray and sauté the mushrooms and spring onion for 2-3 minutes until soft. Place in a bowl.
2. Pre-heat the grill to high.
3. Allow the mushrooms to cool slightly, then add the grated cheese, mustard powder, Henderson's relish and egg yolk. Add a little freshly ground black pepper to taste.
4. Slice the muffins and place them cut side down on a baking sheet. Pop them under the grill and toast the bottoms until golden and crisp.
5. Turn the muffins over, but don't toast the top side yet! Reduce the grill to medium.
6. Spread the cheese and mushroom mixture evenly over the tops of the muffins and pop back under the grill for 2-3 minutes until the cheese has melted and gone golden.

Apple Pie Porridge

PREP TIME 5 COOK TIME 7 SERVINGS 3

Ingredients

- 80 g rolled porridge oats
- 550 ml oat milk
- 2 medium red eating apples skins left on and coarsely grated
- ¼ tsp ground cinnamon
- pinch of ground nutmeg
- 1 tbsp honey
- 1 tsp vanilla extract

For the top
- 9 thin slices of red eating apple skin left on
- 2 tsp honey
- 1 tbsp flaked almonds
- low calorie cooking spray

Instructions

1. Place the oats, oat milk, grated apple, cinnamon, nutmeg, honey and vanilla extract in a medium saucepan and stir well.
2. Place over a medium heat and bring to the boil. Reduce the heat to low and simmer gently for 6-7 minutes, stirring until thickened and the oats have softened.
3. For the top
4. Spray a small frying pan with low calorie cooking spray and place over a medium heat. Add the apple slices and flaked almonds and cook for 1-2 minutes on all sides, until golden and the apples are slightly tender. Stir in the honey to glaze the apple slices and flaked almonds.
5. Place the porridge in 3 bowls and place 3 slices of glazed apple, with a few almonds, on top of each. Serve at once, alone or with an accompaniment of your choice.

Banana and Maple Porridge

PREP TIME 5   COOK TIME 10   SERVINGS 3

Ingredients

For the porridge
- 80 g rolled porridge oats
- 550 ml coconut dairy free milk alternative
- 3 tbsp desiccated coconut
- 1 tbsp maple syrup
- 1 tsp vanilla extract
- pinch of ground ginger

For the topping
- 1 small banana, peeled and sliced
- 1 tbsp maple syrup
- 1 tbsp desiccated coconut

Instructions

1. Place the oats, coconut milk alternative, desiccated coconut, maple syrup, vanilla extract and ginger in a medium saucepan and stir well.
2. Place over a medium heat and bring to the boil. Reduce the heat to low and simmer gently for 6-7 minutes, stirring until thickened and the oats have softened.
3. For the topping: Preheat the grill on a medium setting. Place the coconut in a small ovenproof dish and place under the grill. Toast the coconut for 1-2 minutes or until golden, turning once and watching carefully as it can burn very easily.
4. Place the porridge in three bowls and place a few slices of banana on top of each. Drizzle over the maple syrup and sprinkle with toasted coconut. Serve at once, alone or with an accompaniment of your choice.

Strawberry Oat Muffins

PREP TIME 5   COOK TIME 35   SERVINGS 6

Ingredients

- 80 g oats
- 115 g fat free strawberry yoghurt
- 1 tsp strawberry essence
- 3 medium eggs
- 1½ tbsp granulated sweetener
- 6 fresh strawberries washed, dried and stalks removed
- low calorie cooking spray

Instructions

1. Pre-heat oven 180°C
2. Spray a 6 hole muffin tray (silicone works best) with low calorie cooking spray
3. Mix together oats, eggs and yoghurt
4. Add sweetener and strawberry essence and mix well
5. Spoon mixture into your muffin tray
6. Gently push a strawberry into each muffin
7. Pop into the oven and bake for 30-35 minutes

Air Fryer Full English

PREP TIME 10 **COOK TIME** 20 **SERVINGS** 4

Ingredients

- 8 bacon medallions
- 4 reduced fat pork sausages
- 4 medium eggs beaten
- 420 g tin of baked beans
- 200 g cherry tomatoes
- 200 g button mushrooms
- low calorie cooking spray
- salt and pepper to taste

Instructions

1. Pre-heat your air fryer to 180°C.
2. Take a sheet of foil and place the mushrooms onto it. Spray with low calorie cooking spray and season with salt and pepper. Scrunch the edges together to seal it into a pouch. It should look like a pasty that has been stood up.
3. Take a sheet of foil and place the tomatoes onto it. Spray with low calorie cooking spray and season with salt and pepper. Scrunch it into a pouch.
4. Place the sausages and foil pouches into the air fryer for 5 minutes.
5. After 5 minutes, add the bacon medallions. You will need to overlap them to fit in most air fryers - this is fine!
6. After another 5 minutes, open the air fryer and push the bacon into a pile to make room. Add two small ovenproof bowls, one with the baked beans and one with the beaten eggs. Close the air fryer and cook for another 5 minutes.
7. Open the air fryer again and mix the eggs with a fork, close the lid and cook for a further 2 minutes.
8. Turn off the air fryer and mix up the eggs. Plate up the breakfasts and serve!

Strawberry Souffle Omelette

PREP TIME 10 **COOK TIME** 5 **SERVINGS** 1

Ingredients

- 2 eggs yolk and white separated
- 1 tsp granulated sweetener
- 5 strawberries (around 65g) stalks removed and sliced
- 1 tsp reduced sugar strawberry jam
- 1/8 tsp icing sugar for dusting
- low calorie cooking spray

Instructions

1. Spray an ovenproof frying pan with low calorie cooking spray and grease thoroughly. Mix the strawberries with the jam and set aside.
2. Place the egg yolks and sweetener in a large bowl and beat with an electric whisk for 1 - 2 minutes, until well combined. The mixture will still be runny at this stage.
3. Wash the whisks in hot soapy water and dry thoroughly before proceeding.
4. Place the egg whites in a mixing bowl and whisk until stiff peaks have formed.
5. Tip the whisked egg whites into the egg yolk mixture and, using a large metal spoon, fold in until just combined. Take care not to knock the air out of the mixture.
6. Place the greased frying pan on a medium heat. When hot, tip in the egg mixture and gently spread out to a diameter of approximately 15cm. Preheat the grill on a medium setting.
7. Cook the omelette in the frying pan for 2 - 3 minutes, or until the edges start to dry. Carefully lift the edge to look underneath, the base should be light golden.
8. Place the omelette in the frying pan under the preheated grill, and grill for 1 - 2 minutes until the top is light golden brown.
9. Transfer the omelette to a serving plate.
10. Place the strawberry mixture on one half of the omelette and fold the other half over the top. Dust with the icing sugar and serve at once.

Pizza Waffles

PREP TIME 10　　**COOK TIME** 25　　**SERVINGS** 6

Ingredients

For the waffles
- 150 g self raising flour
- 1 medium egg beaten
- 200 ml skimmed milk
- low calorie cooking spray

For the filling
- 200 g passata
- 1 garlic clove crushed
- 5 leaves fresh basil finely chopped
- 30 g reduced fat mozzarella finely chopped
- 20 g reduced fat Cheddar cheese finely grated
- 6 slices pepperoni sliced into strips

For the spicy ketchup dip
- 5 tbsp tomato ketchup
- 1/4 tsp Sriracha

Instructions

1. Pre-heat the oven to 180°C and pre-heat your waffle maker.
2. In a small saucepan add the passata, garlic clove and fresh basil. Heat at a simmer for 5 minutes then leave to one side to cool.
3. In a mixing bowl combine the flour, milk and egg and whisk into a smooth batter.
4. Once your waffle maker is hot spray it with a little low calorie cooking spray.
5. Pour a little of the waffle batter onto the hot plate and spread until it is just covered.
6. Spoon some of the cooled pizza sauce onto the waffle batter then layer with the sliced pepperoni, mozzarella and Cheddar cheese, and top with more of the batter.
7. Seal your waffle maker and cook for 5-6 minutes or until the waffle is crispy and golden brown around the edges.
8. Place the waffles into the preheated oven whilst you cook the other 5 waffles.
9. Once you have made all of your waffles take them out of the oven and cut into finger shapes.
10. In a small bowl mix the ketchup with the Sriracha sauce and serve with the waffles for dipping.

Potato, Cheese and Onion Waffles

PREP TIME 5　　**COOK TIME** 10　　**SERVINGS** 2

Ingredients

- 2 medium potatoes
- 1 tbsp Smash
- ½ tsp garlic powder
- sea salt to taste
- freshly ground black pepper to taste
- 12 g reduced fat Cheddar
- 2 spring onions finely chopped
- low calorie cooking spray

Instructions

In A Waffle Maker

1. Prick the potatoes a few times with a fork. Then cook in the microwave until they're fairly soft
2. Allow them to cool, then peel them
3. Grate the potato into a decent sized bowl, then stir in the Smash, spring onion, garlic powder, grated cheese, salt and pepper
4. Keep stirring until the mix comes together - get your hands in and make it into a ball
5. Turn on the waffle maker and allow it to heat up. Spray with low calorie cooking spray
6. Place the potato mix in the waffle maker, then close the lid and press down to distribute the potato evenly
7. Cook until the waffles are brown and crispy (about 10 minutes or so) then remove from the waffle maker and serve

In a Silicone Waffle Mould

1. Prick the potatoes a few times with a fork. Then cook in the microwave until they're fairly soft
2. Allow them to cool, then peel them
3. Preheat the oven to 200°C
4. Grate the potato into a decent sized bowl, then stir in the Smash, spring onion, garlic powder, grated cheese, salt and pepper
5. Keep stirring until the mix comes together - get your hands in and make it into a ball
6. Spray your waffle mould with low calorie cooking spray
7. Place the potato mix in the waffle mould and put in the oven for 20 minutes
8. Remove the waffle from the mould, flip over and return to the oven for a further 10-15 minutes until it's browned & serve

BLT Sandwich

PREP TIME 5 **COOK TIME** 10 **SERVINGS** 1

Ingredients

- 3 slices wholemeal bread taken from a 400g loaf
- 2 bacon medallions
- 2 eggs
- 1 medium sized tomato sliced
- 2 lettuce leaves
- 1 tbsp tomato ketchup
- 1 tbsp lighter than light mayonnaise
- low calorie cooking spray

Instructions

1. First weigh the 3 slices of bread. If it is over 60g cut off some of the crust from 1 slice and weigh it again, until you get 60g.
2. Spray a frying pan with low calorie cooking spray and cook the bacon and eggs. You'll want the eggs quite hard so they don't make a mess when you eat the BLT.
3. If you want, you can toast the bread at this point.
4. Lay out the bread with the slice you cut the crust off in the middle.
5. Spread half of the ketchup onto one of the bigger slices of bread then place the eggs on top. Spread a little of the light mayo onto one side of the smaller slice of bread and stack on-top of the ketchup and egg slice.
6. Spread the top piece of bread with a little more of the mayo, then add the bacon, sliced tomato and lettuce. Put the remaining mayo on the last piece of bread.
7. Place this slice on top of the lettuce and cut the sandwich in half diagonally. Enjoy!

Pie Overnight Oats

PREP TIME 10   **SERVINGS** 1

Ingredients

For the Oat Layer
- 37 g porridge oats
- 100 g fat free natural yoghurt
- 1 small apple grated
- 1 handful blackcurrants
- 1 tsp granulated sweetener
- ¼ tsp vanilla extract

For the Custard Layer
- 80 g fat free natural yoghurt
- 50 g quark
- 1 tsp vanilla extract
- ½ tsp chia seeds
- 1 tsp granulated sweetener

Instructions

1. Mix together the oats, yoghurt, grated apple, granulated sweetener and vanilla extract
2. Place this mixture in the bottom of a Kilner jar (the jar should be able to hold up to 350ml)
3. Spread the blackcurrants over the top of this layer
4. In a clean bowl, mix together the "custard" ingredients - yoghurt, quark, vanilla extract, chia seeds and granulated sweetener. Beat it well to remove any lumps. You could add a drop of yellow food colouring to add a custardy colour.
5. Pour this mixture on top of the blackcurrants, close the lid and refrigerate overnight

Courgette and Butter Bean Frittata

PREP TIME 10   **COOK TIME** 20   **SERVINGS** 4

Ingredients

- 4 eggs
- 1 onion diced
- 2 cloves garlic chopped
- 1 large courgette sliced
- 1 can butter beans drained and rinsed - or you could use cannelini or borlotti beans
- 1/2 tin chopped tomatoes drained well, or 3 fresh tomatoes, skinned and chopped
- 2 spring onions
- 40 g low fat cheddar grated
- low calorie cooking spray
- sea salt
- freshly ground black pepper

Instructions

1. Heat the low calorie cooking spray in a large frying pan and fry the onions and garlic until soft.
2. Add the courgette and cook until they are softened, remove from heat.
3. Crack the eggs into a large bowl, season and mix well.
4. Add the fried vegetables, butter beans and tomatoes and stir.
5. Spray the pan with a bit more low calorie cooking spray and heat the pan.
6. Add the egg mixture and cook on a medium heat for 5 minutes or so, until the eggs have almost set and the bottom is browned.
7. Sprinkle the grated cheese evenly over the top and put under a pre heated grill for 3-5 minutes until set on top but still moist in the middle. Cut into 8 wedges and serve 2 per portion.

Sausage Hash

PREP TIME 10　　**COOK TIME** 30　　**SERVINGS** 2

Ingredients

- 1 large potato diced
- 1 pepper diced
- 1 red onion diced
- 1 courgette slice
- 4 low fat sausages cooked and sliced
- 2 eggs
- low calorie cooking spray
- Schwartz Season All

Instructions

1. Wash the potato and cut them into a rough dice, there's no need to peel them. Then put them in a bowl suitable for the microwave and cook them on full power for a few minutes. The potato should still be slightly firm
2. Pre heat the oven to 200°C
3. Spray a large frying pan with low calorie cooking spray, heat until it starts to sizzle and add the diced onion, peppers and potato. Sprinkle with a little Season All, then cook until they just start to colour
4. Add the courgettes and sausage and continue to cook until the veg is browned
5. Divide the mixture equally between 2 oven proof dishes and make a shallow well in each one
6. Crack an egg into each well and cook in the oven for about 12 minutes, until the egg is set (12 minutes will give you a runny egg, so if you prefer a harder yolk leave it in for couple of extra minutes)

Breakfast Bake

PREP TIME 10 **COOK TIME** 20 **SERVINGS** 2

Ingredients

- 2 medium eggs
- 200 g tinned chopped tomatoes
- 2 cooked reduced fat sausages, sliced
- ½ medium onion, peeled and diced
- 4 mushrooms, sliced
- 20 g reduced fat Cheddar, finely grated
- salt and pepper, to taste
- low calorie cooking spray

Instructions

1. Preheat the oven to 190°C and spray oven dishes or ramekins with low calorie cooking spray.
2. Spray a frying pan with low calorie cooking spray and set on a medium heat. Add the onions and cook for 3-4 minutes, add the mushrooms and fry for a further 3-4 minutes. The onions and mushrooms should be soft and starting to brown.
3. Divide the sliced sausage, onions and mushrooms evenly between the two dishes.
4. Spoon the chopped tomatoes over the onions and mushrooms.
5. Season to taste with salt and pepper and sprinkle over the cheese.
6. Crack an egg on the top of each one, spray with a little low calorie cooking spray and season with a little more salt and pepper.
7. Bake in the oven for 15-20 minutes until the egg is cooked and serve.

English Pinwheels

PREP TIME 10 **COOK TIME** 30 **SERVINGS** 16

Ingredients

- 375 g sheet reduced-fat puff pastry
- 2 reduced-fat pork sausages
- 200 g tin baked beans
- 4 mushrooms, diced
- 2 medium eggs, beaten
- 1 tsp skimmed milk
- salt and pepper, to taste
- low-calorie cooking spray

Instructions

1. Preheat the oven to 180°C and line a baking tray with non-stick baking paper.
2. Spray a frying pan with low-calorie cooking spray and set on a medium heat. Add the sausages to one side of the pan and mushrooms to the other. Fry for 10 minutes, turning the sausages to get an even colouring. The mushrooms should release all the moisture and be a golden brown colour.
3. Cook the egg in the microwave in 1 minute bursts until cooked and scrambled. It should have more of a firm texture and not be too wet. Leave to one side to cool slightly.
4. Once cooked, dice the sausages and leave to one side to cool slightly.
5. Unroll the pastry sheet, leaving it on the greaseproof paper packaging, and place on your work surface.
6. Spoon over the beans, trying to get an even coverage. Add the diced sausage, mushrooms and scrambled egg. Season to taste with salt and pepper.
7. Roll-up the pastry, starting with the long edge closest to you, using the greaseproof paper packaging to help you.
8. Keep rolling until you have made a 'Swiss roll'. When you have finished rolling the pastry up, make sure it is seam side down.
9. Use a large, serrated knife to cut into 16 spiral-shaped slices.
10. Place the swirls flat onto the lined baking tray, leaving gaps between each swirl and brush with skimmed milk.
11. Place the tray into the oven for 20-25 minutes, until the swirls are golden and crisp. Place on a cooling rack to cool or serve warm fresh from the oven.

Peanut Butter and Jelly Baked Oats

PREP TIME 5   COOK TIME 40   SERVINGS 1

Ingredients

- 40 g rolled oats
- 175 g fat-free natural yoghurt
- 1 medium egg
- 1 tbsp peanut butter powder
- 1 tbsp white granulated sweetener
- 1 tsp reduced-sugar strawberry jam

Instructions

1. Preheat the oven to 180°C.
2. Add the yoghurt, peanut butter powder, sweetener and egg to a mixing bowl and mix until smooth and combined.
3. Add the oats and mix until combined with the yoghurt mixture.
4. Pour the oat mixture into an ovenproof dish and place the jam in the middle of the oats.
5. Place the dish onto a baking tray and bake for 35-40 minutes until risen. Remove from the oven and serve.

Berry Toastie

PREP TIME 5   COOK TIME 4   SERVINGS 1

Ingredients

- 2 slices of Danish Lighter white bread
- 40 g frozen mixed berries, defrosted
- 2 tbsp low-fat cream cheese
- 1 tsp reduced-fat spread
- 1 tsp white granulated sweetener
- ½ tsp icing sugar
- ½ tsp maple syrup
- low-calorie cooking spray

Instructions

1. Add the cream cheese and sweetener to a small bowl and mix until combined.
2. Spread one side of each slice of bread with the reduced-fat spread. Flip the bread over and spread the cream cheese onto both slices.
3. Arrange the fruit on one slice of bread and place the other piece of bread on top, with the cream cheese side facing inwards.
4. Spray a frying pan with low-calorie cooking spray and set on a low heat. When the pan is hot, add the toastie and cook for 1-2 minutes. Flip and cook for a further 1-2 minutes. The bread should be golden brown and crispy.
5. Remove the toastie from the pan and cut in half. Dust with icing sugar and drizzle over the maple syrup. Serve.

Rainbow Waffles

PREP TIME 5 **COOK TIME** 12 **SERVINGS** 2

Ingredients

- 150 g self-raising flour
- 200 ml skimmed milk
- 1 medium egg
- 1 tsp white granulated sweetener
- 1 orange zested
- low-calorie cooking spray

To serve
- 80 g fat-free Greek yoghurt
- 1 orange
- 1 grapefruit
- 2 tsp honey

Instructions

1. Preheat your waffle maker.
2. Add the flour to a large mixing bowl along with the milk, egg, sweetener and orange zest. Mix with a balloon whisk until fully combined and you have a smooth batter. Leave the batter to one side while your waffle maker preheats.
3. Once your waffle maker is hot, spray it with a little low-calorie cooking spray.
4. Pour half of the waffle batter onto the hot plate and spread out. It depends on the size of your waffle maker; we made 2 large circle waffles with 4 waffle sections in each circle.
5. Seal your waffle maker and cook for 5-6 minutes, or until the waffle is crispy and golden brown around the edges.
6. Place the waffles onto a plate and cover with foil to keep warm, while you cook the other waffles.
7. Prepare the fruit. Using a sharp knife, remove the ends and discard – this will give you a flat surface on each end. Stand the fruit upright on one of the flat ends, and cut away a section of the peel from the top, all the way around the fruit down to the chopping board. Be sure to remove all the white pith.
8. Make slices down and around the edges to remove all the peel of the orange and grapefruit. Lay the orange and grapefruit on the side and slice into slices of your preferred thickness.
9. Stack up the waffles on your serving plates. Top with a dollop of yoghurt, orange and grapefruit slices, and a drizzle of honey.

Sunshine Pancakes

PREP TIME 10   **COOK TIME** 20   **SERVINGS** 2

Ingredients

- For the pancakes
- 50 g coconut flour
- 3 eggs
- 100 ml plant-based coconut milk alternative, eg. Alpro or Koko
- ½ tsp baking powder
- 1 tbsp granulated sweetener
- ½ tsp vanilla essence
- For the topping
- 160 g fresh pineapple, peeled and diced
- juice of half a lime
- 1 tbsp water
- 100 g fat-free Greek yoghurt
- low-calorie cooking spray

Instructions

1. Whisk the eggs, coconut milk and sweetener together in a jug and add the vanilla essence.
2. Place the coconut flour and baking powder in a mixing bowl and stir well. Gradually add the egg mixture and whisk until smooth. Cover and leave to rest for 15 minutes while you prepare the topping.
3. Spray a small pan with low-calorie cooking spray and place on a medium heat. Add the pineapple, lime juice, water and 1 tbsp of sweetener to the pan and cook for 10 minutes until the liquid has reduced to a sticky glaze. Set aside.
4. Place a large nonstick frying pan onto a medium heat, spray with low-calorie cooking spray and allow it to become hot.
5. Coconut flour can vary in absorbency from brand to brand, so check your pancake batter. It should have thickened while resting. You want a spoonable consistency, rather than a pouring one. If the batter is too thin add a little extra coconut flour, if it is too thick and some extra coconut milk.
6. Using half the mixture, spoon 3 pancakes, about 8-10 cm in diameter, into the frying pan. Don't make them too big as they can be quite delicate to flip. Cook for 2-3 minutes, until the bottom is golden and the edges are starting to set. Using a wide spatula, carefully flip the pancakes and continue cooking for a further 1-2 minutes. Stack onto a plate then cook your second batch.
7. Serve 3 pancakes per portion, stacked onto plates and topped with the caramelised pineapple and a spoonful of yoghurt on the side.

Breakfast Wrap

PREP TIME 20 **COOK TIME** 20 **SERVINGS** 2

Ingredients

- 1 reduced-fat sausage
- 2 smoked bacon medallions
- 1 potato peeled approx. 120g
- 2 reduced-fat processed cheese slices
- 2 low-calorie soft tortilla wraps
- 1 medium egg
- ¼ tsp garlic granules
- ¼ tsp onion granules
- ¼ tsp dried sage
- 2 tsp ketchup or brown sauce
- salt and pepper to taste
- low-calorie cooking spray

Instructions

1. Place the potato into a small saucepan and cover with boiling water. Cook for 6 minutes until just starting to soften. Run the saucepan under cold water until the potato is cold enough to handle.
2. Grate the potato and divide the mixture in half. Shape into two rectangle hash brown shapes. Spray a frying pan with low-calorie cooking spray and set on a medium heat. Add the hash browns and cook for 4 minutes on each side until golden brown.
3. While the hash browns are cooking, squeeze the sausage into a small bowl. Add the garlic granules, onion granules, sage and season with salt and pepper. Mix the mixture with your hands until smooth and shape into two rectangle sausage patties.
4. Spray a frying pan with low-calorie cooking spray and set on a medium heat. Add the sausage patties and bacon to the pan and cook the first side for 3 minutes. Flip over and cook the other side for 3 minutes.
5. Once the sausage patties and bacon are cooked, remove from the pan and place onto a plate. Cover with foil to keep warm while you prepare the egg.
6. Beat the egg in a small bowl with 1 tbsp water, season with salt and pepper. Wipe out the frying pan and spray with a little more low-calorie cooking spray and set on a medium heat. Pour in the egg and swirl the pan until the egg is spread out into a thin omelette.
7. Flip the egg over after 2 minutes and cook for a further 2 minutes until golden. Microwave the tortilla wraps for 30 seconds until they are warm.
8. Now you are ready to assemble the breakfast wraps. Spread each wrap with a little brown sauce or ketchup.
9. Cut the egg in half and lay each half onto the top half of the tortilla wrap. Add a slice of cheese, bacon medallion, hash brown and then the sausage patty.
10. Fold the bottom half of the tortilla wrap over the filling, then fold the two edges over each other and enjoy!

Overnight Oats

PREP TIME 5 **COOK TIME** overnight **SERVINGS** 1

Ingredients

- 40 g Rolled porridge oats
- 200 g fat free yoghurt (if you aren't using a flavoured yoghurt, you may want to add some sweetener or honey)
- 2 handfuls mixed frozen berries

Instructions

1. Put one handful of berries into the bottom of your jar/bowl
2. sprinkle over half the oats
3. spoon over half of the yoghurt
4. Repeat, so you have another layer of everything
5. Pop into the fridge and leave overnight for the magic to happen!

Chocolate Overnight Weetabix

PREP TIME 5 **COOK TIME** overnight **SERVINGS** 1

Ingredients

- 2 Weetabix, crumbled up
- 1.5 tbsp coco powder or chocolate powder
- 118.50 ml skimmed milk (enough to make the Weetabix into a base)
- 1 fat free chocolate protein yogurt (or mix some chocolate powder into a vanilla one)
- 19 g chocolate spread, melted.
- 1 banana or fruit of your choice sliced

Instructions

1. Add the crumbled up weetabix to a resealable container
2. Mix in the coco powder and milk, mix well then press down to create a base.
3. Add the yogurt and spread out until its smooth
4. Drizzle with the chocolate spread and the fruit of your choice.
5. Leave in the fridge overnight!

Note
You can use any fruit of your choice to top these dishes.

Soups & Salads

Carrot, Orange and Thyme Soup

PREP TIME 10   COOK TIME 35   SERVINGS 4

Ingredients

- 450 g carrots peeled and finely chopped
- 2 medium onions peeled and finely chopped
- 1 clove garlic peeled and crushed
- 1 vegetable stock pot
- 1 litre boiling water
- 2 tsp fresh thyme leaves finely chopped
- 200 ml fresh orange juice
- low calorie cooking spray
- salt and freshly ground black pepper, to taste

Instructions

1. Spray a large saucepan with low calorie cooking spray and place on a medium heat.
2. Add the onions and garlic and fry for 10 minutes, stirring, until golden and softened slightly.
3. Add the carrots, stock pot dissolved in boiling water and thyme, cover and simmer over a low heat for 25 minutes until the carrots and onions are tender.
4. Carefully transfer to a food processor and blitz until smooth. You may need to do this in two batches. Alternatively, use a handheld stick blender.
5. Transfer the soup back to the saucepan. Stir in the orange juice and season to taste with salt and pepper.
6. If needed, heat, uncovered over a low heat for 2 –3 minutes until piping hot and serve.

Mulligatawny Soup

PREP TIME 15 **COOK TIME** 35 **SERVINGS** 6

Ingredients

- 2 onions chopped
- 2 peppers cut into 1cm pieces
- 3 carrots peeled and diced into 1cm pieces
- 75 g butternut squash peeled and diced into 1cm pieces
- 75 g red lentils
- 50 g basmati rice
- 2 cloves garlic peeled and crushed
- 2 tbsp curry powder mild or hot depending on your taste
- 1 tin 400g chopped tomatoes
- 3 vegetable stock cubes made up with 1.75ltr of boiling water
- 2 tbsp tomato puree
- ½ lemon, juice only
- 10 g fresh coriander leaves chopped
- 3 tbsp fat free Greek yogurt
- low calorie cooking spray

Instructions

1. Spray a large saucepan with low calorie cooking spray, place over a medium heat and sauté the onions and peppers for 3-4 minutes, until they are beginning to soften.
2. Add the garlic and curry powder, and cook for another minute, allowing the spices to become fragrant.
3. Add the carrots, butternut squash and lentils to the pan, then stir in the stock, tomatoes and tomato puree.
4. Bring the soup to the boil, then reduce the heat and simmer for 10 minutes.
5. Add the rice and continue cooking for a further 20 minutes, until the vegetables are soft.
6. At this point, you can blend the soup if you wish, but we prefer it chunkier, so take a fork or a masher and lightly crush some of the butternut squash. This will thicken the soup, while keeping a chunkier texture.
7. Stir through the yogurt, lemon juice and coriander and serve in a warmed bowl.

Pea and Ham Soup

PREP TIME 10 COOK TIME 30 SERVINGS 6

Ingredients

- 750 g gammon joint all fat removed
- 250 g dried peas we use Quick Soak
- 2 ham stock cubes or chicken - Dissolved in 400ml of boiling water
- 6 carrots peeled and cut into thick even slices
- 1 onion cut into large dice
- 3 sticks celery cut into chunks
- 1 bay leaf
- low calorie cooking spray

Instructions

Stove top method
1. Remove any fat from the ham and place in a large pan.
2. Add the carrots, onion, celery and bay leaf.
3. Cover with water, bring to the boil and simmer for approx 2 hours.
4. Soak the peas. If you're using quick soak then they will be ready when the ham is cooked. If not, then don't forget to soak the peas overnight.
5. Remove the ham and veg from the liquid, fish out the bayleaf and reserve the remaining cooking liquid.
6. Wash and drain the peas and add them to a clean pan.
7. Cut the cooked ham into cubes.
8. If you prefer your soups chunky, add half of the diced ham and veg to the pan with the peas, then add enough of the ham cooking liquid to cover the ingredients. If you like a smooth soup add *all* the chopped up ham and veg at this point
9. Add the stock cubes, bring up to the boil then simmer for around 20 minutes.
10. Check the peas are soft, then blend the soup with a stick blender until it's smooth.
11. If you reserved some ham and veg, return it to the pan and leave on the heat for a few minutes until it's heated through. If the soup is a little thick, just add a bit more water or ham stock until it reaches the desired consistency

Instant Pot method
1. Make sure you pre-soak the peas before you start. 2 hours if using Quick Soak or overnight if using regular dried peas.

2. Set the Instant Pot to sauté and spray with some low calorie cooking spray.
3. Brown the ham on all sides then set aside.
4. Add the onion, celery and half of the sliced carrots. Sauté until the veg starts to colour.
5. Return the ham to the Instant Pot and add the made up stock and the bay leaf.
6. Replace the lid and set to manual for 15 minutes (natural pressure release - NPR).
7. Remove the bay leaf and add the soaked peas, then cook on manual for 10 minutes (NPR).
8. Add the reserved carrots and another 300ml of water.
9. Set to manual for 5 minutes (NPR).
10. If you like a smooth soup, you can blitz the soup using a stick blender or food processor.
11. If you prefer your soup chunky, remove half of the meat and veg chunks from the soup and set aside, then blitz the soup until smooth. If it's a little too thick, add some more water or stock until it reaches the desired consistency
12. Return the reserved chunks to the Instant Pot and stir well and set to keep warm until you're ready to serve.

Slow cooker method
1. Soak the peas according to packet instructions.
2. Remove any fat from the ham and place in the slow cooker along with all the other ingredients.
3. Cook on High for 6 hours.
4. Once the ham is falling apart, take some of the ham out, remove the bay leaf and then blitz the soup until it reaches your desired constancy. Add the reserved ham back into the soup and serve.

Curried parsnip Soup

PREP TIME 15 **COOK TIME** 20 **SERVINGS** 4

Ingredients

- 3 parsnips peeled
- 1 large potato, approx. 200g, peeled and chopped into chunks
- 2 cloves garlic peeled and crushed
- 1 medium onion peeled and diced
- 1-2 tbsp medium curry powder (use hot or mild if preferred)
- 1 vegetable stock pot
- 10 g fresh coriander
- 1½ l boiling water
- low-calorie cooking spray

Instructions

1. Keep half of one parsnip aside. Chop the rest of the parsnips into 1 inch pieces. Add to a saucepan with the potato, garlic, onion, curry powder and stock pot. Stir in the boiling water and simmer for 10 minutes.
2. Chop the half parsnip you put aside, into ½cm dice. Add to an air fryer with some low-calorie cooking spray and air-fry at 180°C for 10 minutes until crisp.
3. After 10 minutes, finely chop the leafy part of the fresh coriander and add half to the saucepan. Simmer for a further 10 minutes.
4. Transfer the vegetables to a food processor or use a stick blender to blitz until thick and creamy. You may need to add some extra boiling water if it is too thick. Add the remaining coriander leaves and blitz for a further few seconds.
5. Serve immediately, topped with the parsnip croutons and a sprinkle of extra curry powder.

Tomato Soup & Croutons

PREP TIME 10 **COOK TIME** 50 **SERVINGS** 6

Ingredients

- 2 medium onions peeled and sliced
- 2 sticks celery chopped
- 2 carrots peeled and chopped
- 4 cloves garlic crushed
- 2 tins chopped tomatoes, 400g/14oz tin
- 1 tin butter beans, 400g/14oz tin drained
- 400 g cauliflower florets roughly chopped
- ½ tsp dried basil
- 1 tbsp balsamic vinegar
- 2 vegetable stock cubes
- 800 ml boiling water to make the vegetable stock
- 1 tbsp Henderson's Relish or Worcestershire sauce
- low calorie cooking spray
- salt and pepper to taste

For the croutons
- 2 gluten free ciabatta rolls e.g. Schar branded
- 1 tsp garlic granules
- low calorie cooking spray

Instructions

For the soup
1. Add the onion, celery, carrot and garlic cloves to a large saucepan and spray with low calorie cooking spray. Gently fry over a medium heat for 10 minutes, until softened.
2. Add the tinned tomatoes, butter beans, cauliflower, basil, balsamic vinegar, stock and Henderson's Relish to the saucepan. Reduce the heat and simmer for 40 minutes with a lid on the pan, stirring occasionally.
3. When ready, blend the soup until smooth. If you need to add extra water at this point you can do so. Season with salt and pepper to taste.

For the croutons
1. Whilst the soup is simmering, slice each of the bread rolls into 3 slices down the middle. Cut each slice into cubes.
2. Add the bread cubes to a frying pan. Coat with low calorie cooking spray and sprinkle over garlic granules. Toast over a medium heat for 5 minutes, until the bread is crispy.
3. Serve the soup with some croutons sprinkled on top.

Broccoli and Stilton Soup

PREP TIME 10   COOK TIME 25   SERVINGS 6

Ingredients

- 500 g potatoes, peeled and quartered
- 1 head of broccoli approx 350g, broken into florets and stalks roughly chopped
- 2 large onions, peeled and sliced
- 70 g Stilton or blue cheese, crumbled
- 2 garlic cloves, peeled and minced
- 1 L vegetable stock, made of 2 vegetable stock cubes and 1L boiling water
- low calorie cooking spray
- salt and pepper to taste

Instructions

1. Spray a large saucepan with low calorie cooking spray and place over a medium heat. Add the onions, garlic and chopped broccoli stalk and cook for 5 minutes until the onion begins to soften.
2. Add the potato, broccoli florets and stock. Bring to the boil and then reduce to a simmer and place the lid on the saucepan for 15 minutes. When it's ready the potatoes will be tender.
3. Remove the lid and add the Stilton. Stir until it has melted.
4. Remove the pan from the heat and blitz the soup with a hand blender until smooth.
5. Season with salt and pepper to taste and serve

Red Pepper and Feta Soup

PREP TIME 15　　**COOK TIME** 45　　**SERVINGS** 6

Ingredients

- 6 red peppers halved and seeds removed
- 1 large onion roughly chopped
- 8 tomatoes quartered
- 6 cloves of garlic
- 3 vegetable stock cubes made up with 1.75l of boiling water
- 2 tbsp balsamic vinegar
- 1 tbsp Henderson's Relish
- 2 tbsp tomato puree
- 100 g reduced fat feta
- low calorie cooking spray

Instructions

1. Preheat the oven to 200°C.
2. Place the peppers (skin side up), onion, tomatoes and garlic on a baking sheet (you may need to use 2 trays) and roast in the oven for 30 minutes, until the peppers are soft and have charred.
3. Put all the roasted vegetables and all remaining ingredients, except the feta, into a large saucepan with the stock.
4. Stir well and bring to a boil, then reduce the heat and allow to simmer uncovered for 15 minutes.
5. Remove from the heat, stir through half of the feta and, using a stick blender, blitz until smooth, being careful not to splash yourself with hot soup!
6. Ladle into warmed bowls and sprinkle a little feta on top, along with some fresh herbs if you wish.

Spinach and Rocket Soup

PREP TIME 10   **COOK TIME** 20   **SERVINGS** 4

Ingredients

- 100 g spinach
- 70 g rocket
- 1 onion chopped
- 2 cloves garlic crushed
- 200 g potato peeled and cut into 2.5cm/ 1" chunks
- 2 vegetable stock cubes
- 650 ml boiling water
- ½ lemon juice only
- 30 g parmesan cheese grated
- 5 fresh basil leaves
- 250 ml oat milk or skimmed milk
- salt and freshly ground black pepper
- low calorie cooking spray

Instructions

1. Spray the pan with low calorie cooking spray.
2. Over a medium heat, sauté the onions for 5 minutes, until soft. Add the garlic and continue cooking for another minute.
3. Pour in the stock and oat milk, then add the potatoes and lemon juice. Stir well and bring to the boil.
4. Reduce the heat and allow to simmer gently for 20 minutes, until the potatoes are cooked.
5. Add the rocket, spinach and basil leaves and allow a minute or 2 for them to wilt.
6. Stir in the grated parmesan and then pour into a blender (or use a stick blender) and blitz to a soup.
7. Return to the pan, add a little salt and freshly ground black pepper to taste.
8. Return the pan to the heat to ensure the soup is piping hot and then serve in warm bowls.

White Onion Soup

PREP TIME 15　**COOK TIME** 45　**SERVINGS** 4

Ingredients

- 1 kg white onions peeled and sliced
- 200 g half fat crème fraiche
- 3 sprigs fresh thyme
- 1 chicken stock pot
- 1 white wine stock pot
- 850 ml water
- salt and pepper to taste
- low calorie cooking spray

Instructions

1. Spray a saucepan with low calorie cooking spray and set on a medium heat. Add the onions and cook for 25-30 minutes, stirring frequently to prevent colouring.
2. Add the chicken stock pot, white wine stock pot, water and thyme and bring to a simmer, then reduce heat and continue cooking for 15 minutes.
3. Remove the thyme sprigs, then blitz the soup with a stick blender until smooth. Add the crème fraiche, then season to taste with salt and pepper before serving.

Chicken Teriyaki Noodle Soup

PREP TIME 5 **COOK TIME** 5 **SERVINGS** 1

Ingredients

- 1 Japanese Teriyaki Naked Noodle Pot
- 2 spring onions chopped
- 2 or 3 mushrooms sliced
- 1 clove garlic finely chopped
- 1 piece fresh ginger (about the size of £1 coin) finely chopped
- 200 ml chicken stock
- 1/2 cooked chicken breast cut into small pieces
- 1 medium carrot cut into thin strips

Instructions

1. Add boiling water to the Naked Noodle pot.
2. Cover and allow to stand for 2 minutes, then stir.
3. Meanwhile, heat up a wok or frying pan. Spray with low calorie cooking spray.
4. Sauté the spring onion, ginger, garlic, mushrooms and carrots for a few minutes.
5. Add the chicken and stock. Allow to simmer for 30-40 seconds.
6. Stir in the Naked Noodle Pot and serve topped with some more finely chopped spring onion.

Rice Noodle Soup

PREP TIME 2 **COOK TIME** 8 **SERVINGS** 2

Ingredients

- 1 bag stir fry veg
- 100 g rice noodles
- 750 ml vegetable stock
- 1 chilli deseeded and chopped
- 1/2 lime
- 1 stalk lemongrass bashed with the back of a knife until it is roughly crushed
- 1 tsp Lazy Garlic
- 2 tsp Lazy Ginger
- low calorie cooking spray

Instructions

1. Fry the chilli, garlic, ginger and the lemongrass stalk for a minute or so in a little low calorie cooking spray.
2. Add the veg and fry for a few more minutes.
3. Pour in the stock and add the noodles. Stir and cook for 2-3 minutes until the noodles are cooked.
4. Transfer to serving bowls and squeeze over the juice of the lime.

Salmon Tabbouleh Salad

PREP TIME 20 **COOK TIME** 15 **SERVINGS** 4

Ingredients

- 4 large salmon fillets
- 1/2 tsp ground allspice
- low calorie cooking spray

Basil and yogurt dressing
- 25 g chopped basil
- 120 g 0% greek yogurt
- 10 g chives chopped
- 1 lemon juice of
- 1 tsp granulated sweetener
- 1 tsp onion powder

Tabbouleh
- 150 g bulgar wheat
- 200 g sugar snap peas trimmed and halved
- 10 small radishes sliced
- 1 whole cucumber deseeded & chopped
- 1/2 large red onion chopped finely
- 300 g baby tomatoes
- 1 large red pepper deseeded and sliced
- 25 g flat leaf parsley chopped very finely
- 25 g mint leaves roughly chopped
- Some sprays low calorie cooking spray
- 1 large lemon juice of
- 1/2 tsp ground allspice
- 1 tbsp balsamic vinegar
- 200 ml chicken stock made from boiling water & 1 chicken stock cube

Instructions

1. Start by making the tabbouleh - it can be made a couple of hours ahead of time even! Put the bulgar wheat in a bowl and cover with the chicken stock. Tightly cover the bowl with cling film and set aside for 20 minutes.
2. Whilst waiting for the wheat to soak up the chicken stock, prep the tomatoes, cucumber, radishes, sugar snap peas, pepper, red onion and herbs.
3. After 20 minutes, fluff up the bulgar wheat (it should be al dente - not too soft) and toss in the prepped vegetables and herbs. Whisk together the balsamic, lemon juice and allspice and stir through. Spray periodically with low calorie cooking spray.
4. Spray a a large frying with low calorie cooking spray, and bring up the heat to high. Dust the salmon with the allspice . Fry for 2 minutes, then flip over for another 2 minutes. Place in the oven at 180°C for 10 minutes until cooked.
5. Put the yogurt, herbs, lemon juice and sweetener in a small high speed blender. Season well and whizz up until smooth.
6. Serve the salmon on the tabbouleh, with the dressing along side to drizzle over the salmon.

Chicken and Ham Wraps

PREP TIME 15

SERVINGS 2

Ingredients

- 200 g cooked chicken sliced
- 4 slices cooked ham
- 8 large iceberg lettuce leaves
- 90 g red pepper thinly sliced
- 1 small red onion thinly sliced
- 6 cucumber slices
- 2 tbsp low fat cream cheese
- 1 tomato thinly sliced
- 1 small sprig fresh parsley finely chopped
- salt and black pepper to taste

Instructions

1. Lay 4 of the lettuce leaves overlapping on the greaseproof paper.
2. In a small bowl, mix the low-fat cream cheese, parsley and season to taste with the salt and pepper.
3. Spread the cream cheese mixture evenly over the lettuce then top with the cooked chicken and sliced ham.
4. Add the peppers, cucumber, onion and tomatoes and add more salt and pepper to taste if you like.
5. Roll the greaseproof paper, starting from the longest edge, to form a sausage. Twist each end to seal.
6. To serve, slice diagonally through the middle and keep the halves in the paper.

Kale Salad

PREP TIME 10 COOK TIME 5 SERVINGS 2

Ingredients

- 100 g curly kale
- 150 g fine green beans stalks removed and cut in half
- 150 g green grapes halved and pips removed
- 1 green skinned dessert apple cored and diced
- 50 g watercress
- 100 g ready cooked wholegrain quinoa
- juice of 3 limes (approx 4 tbsp)
- 1 tsp light soy sauce
- 1 tbsp clear honey
- 1/8 tsp garlic granules
- salt and pepper to taste
- lime wedges to garnish optional

Instructions

1. Place a large saucepan of water on the hob and bring to the boil.
2. Add the green beans to the saucepan of boiling water and boil for 3 minutes. Remove the beans from the boiling water using a slotted spoon and plunge into a bowl of cold water.
3. Add the curly kale to the saucepan of boiling water and boil for 2 minutes. Remove the curly kale from the boiling water using a slotted spoon and plunge into a bowl of cold water.
4. Using a sieve, strain off the water from both the beans and the curly kale and shake well to remove excess water. Place on a sheet of kitchen paper to absorb any further moisture.
5. Place the kale and beans in a large bowl and add the grapes, apple, watercress and quinoa.
6. Place the lime juice, soy sauce, honey, and garlic granules in a small bowl. Mix with a fork and season to taste with salt and pepper.
7. Pour the dressing over the salad and toss well. Taste the salad and add a little more salt and pepper if needed.
8. Serve immediately and - optionally - garnish with lime wedges.

Fruit Salad

PREP TIME 15   **COOK TIME** 5   **SERVINGS** 6

Ingredients

- 3 medium oranges peeled and cut into round slices
- 2 medium pink or ruby grapefruits peeled and cut into round slices
- 1 nectarine cut into segments
- 4 fresh figs stalks removed and sliced into round slices
- 100 g blackberries
- 100 g raspberries
- 100 g pomegranate seeds

Instructions

For the orange and honey syrup
1. Place the orange juice, orange zest, honey, cinnamon and nutmeg in a small saucepan and place over a medium heat. Bring to a simmer, then lower the heat and simmer for 4 – 5 minutes, until the orange zest has softened.
2. Remove from the heat, set aside and leave to cool.

For the fruit salad
1. Arrange the oranges, grapefruit, nectarine, figs, blackberries, raspberries and pomegranate seeds on a large serving dish or serving bowl.
2. Pour the cooled orange and honey syrup evenly over the fruit salad, along with the softened orange zest.
3. Sprinkle the pistachio nuts over the top of the fruit salad if wished and serve.

Chickpeas Salad

PREP TIME 15   **COOK TIME** 10   **SERVINGS** 2

Ingredients

- 1 tin chickpeas 400g tin, drained and rinsed
- ½ small red onion finely chopped
- ½ red pepper finely diced
- 1 small mango peeled and cut into small chunks
- 100 g fat free Greek yoghurt
- 2 tsp red wine vinegar
- 2 tsp mild curry powder
- 1 tsp granulated sweetener or sugar
- ½ tsp garlic granules
- a small bunch of coriander chopped
- salt and freshly ground black pepper
- 2-3 tbsp water

Instructions

1. Place the mango in a small saucepan with 2-3 tbsp water and the red wine vinegar. Cover and bring to a simmer over a low heat for 10 minutes or until the mango becomes soft and begins to fall. Riper mangoes will need less cooking than unripe ones.
2. When soft, remove from the heat and set aside for 10 minutes to cool, before blending to a puree.
3. In a large bowl, mix the mango puree with the yoghurt, curry powder, garlic granules and sweetener.
4. Stir in the chickpeas, peppers, onions and coriander.
5. Season to taste with salt and pepper and serve with your choice of accompaniment.

Tabbouleh

PREP TIME 30   **SERVINGS** 6

Ingredients

- 60 g bulgar wheat
- 450 g ripe tomatoes finely diced and drained
- 1 large cucumber finely diced
- 6 spring onions finely chopped
- 60 g flat leaf parsley stalks removed and chopped
- 15 g fresh mint leaves stalks removed and chopped
- 2 lemons juice only
- 5 sprays light olive oil spray
- 80 ml boiling water
- salt and black pepper to taste

Instructions

1. Place the bulgar wheat in a large bowl and pour over 80ml boiling water. Cover with a plate and leave to soak for 20 minutes.
2. Place the diced tomatoes in a sieve over the medium bowl and leave to drain while the bulgar wheat is soaking.
3. When the bulgar wheat has absorbed all of the water, stir with a fork.
4. Add the drained tomatoes, cucumber, spring onion, parsley, mint, and lemon juice to the bulgar wheat. Spray with olive oil spray and mix well with a large spoon. Season to taste with salt and pepper before serving.

Steak and Feta Salad

PREP TIME 5   **COOK TIME** 2   **SERVINGS** 4

Ingredients

For the marinade
- 4 thin cut beef sizzle steaks approx 250g/9oz total weight
- 2 tbsp balsamic vinegar
- 2 tbsp Worcestershire Sauce or Henderson's Relish
- 1 tsp lime juice
- 1 tsp Dijon mustard
- 1 tsp clear honey
- ½ tsp garlic granules
- salt and black pepper to taste

For the salad
- 2 little gem lettuce thinly sliced
- 6 cherry tomatoes quartered
- 4 radishes thinly sliced
- 50 g canned or frozen sweetcorn defrosted and/or drained
- 40 g reduced fat Feta cheese

For the dressing
- 2 tbsp balsamic vinegar
- 1 tbsp lime juice
- 1 tbsp clear honey
- 5 g fresh basil leaves finely chopped
- 5 g flat leafed parsley stalks removed and finely chopped

Instructions

1. In a small bowl, combine all the marinade ingredients and season with a little salt and pepper. Place the steaks in a non-metallic dish and pour over the marinade. Cover with cling film and pop in the fridge for 30 minutes.
2. Arrange the lettuce, cherry tomatoes and radishes on your serving plates, sprinkle over the sweetcorn and crumble over the Feta cheese. It's nice to leave some chunks of Feta so don't break it down too much.
3. In a small bowl, combine the dressing ingredients and leave to one side.
4. Pre-heat the griddle or frying pan and place the steaks in the pan. As the steaks are very thin, a minute on each side will cook them through.
5. Remove from the pan and allow to rest for a minute. Slice the steaks into thin slices and arrange on top of the salad.
6. Drizzle the salad with the dressing and serve.

Vegetable Couscous

PREP TIME 5 COOK TIME 6 SERVINGS 4

Ingredients

- 110 g dried couscous
- 1 small red onion peeled and diced
- ½ red pepper deseeded and diced
- 70 g broccoli chopped into small pieces
- 2 garlic cloves peeled and crushed
- 200 ml boiling water
- ½ vegetable stock cube
- 2 tbsp harissa paste
- 1 tbsp tomato puree
- 30 g reduced-fat feta cheese
- 1 tbsp lime juice
- 5 g mint leaves removed from stalks and finely chopped
- salt and pepper to taste
- low-calorie cooking spray

Instructions

1. Spray a frying pan with low-calorie cooking spray and set on a medium heat.
2. Add the onion and fry for 2 minutes. Add the garlic and peppers and continue to fry for 2 minutes. Add the broccoli and fry for 2 minutes, until starting to soften.
3. To the boiling water, add the stock cube, harissa and tomato puree stir to combine.
4. Remove the pan from the heat and add the couscous into the pan. Stir to mix evenly.
5. Pour the stock mixture into the pan and stir quickly. Cover the pan with foil and leave to stand for 5 minutes.
6. Stir through the mint, lime juice and season with salt and pepper. Crumble over the feta cheese and serve.

Spinach and Chicken Meatball Salad

PREP TIME 15 **COOK TIME** 15 **SERVINGS** 4

Ingredients

For the meatballs
- 3 chicken breasts approx. 400g
- 30 g spinach
- 4 g fresh coriander chopped
- 1 garlic clove peeled and crushed
- 5 cm piece ginger peeled and grated
- ½ red chilli seeds removed and diced
- 1 tbsp lime juice
- 1 tbsp light soy sauce
- 1 tbsp fish sauce
- low-calorie cooking spray

For the dressing
- 4 tbsp cider vinegar
- 2 tbsp reduced sugar and salt tomato ketchup
- 2 tbsp honey
- 2 tbsp lime juice
- ½ tsp Sriracha
- ¼ tsp garlic granules
- ½ red chilli seeds removed and finely diced

For the salad
- 240 g lettuce shredded
- 120 g cucumber sliced
- 8 cherry tomatoes quartered
- Metric - US Customary
- food processor
- Frying pan
- small mixing bowl

Instructions

1. Add the meatball ingredients to a food processor and blitz until smooth.
2. Take walnut-sized amounts of the chicken mixture and roll in your hands to make smooth balls. The mix should make 20 meatballs.
3. Spray a frying pan with low-calorie cooking spray and set on a medium heat. Add the meatballs and cook for 10-12 minutes turning to brown on all sides. Check that the meatballs are cooked by cutting one in half to make sure the juices run clear.
4. While the meatballs are cooking, add the dressing ingredients to a small bowl and stir to combine.
5. Arrange the lettuce, cucumber and tomato on your serving plates top with the meatballs and drizzle with the dressing. Serve.

Beetroot and Rosemary Salad

PREP TIME 15 **COOK TIME** 45 **SERVINGS** 4

Ingredients

- 2 medium fresh raw beetroot approx. 450g (trimmed, peeled and cut into 1½cm chunks)
- 2 tbsp fresh rosemary leaves stalks removed and finely chopped
- juice of 1 medium orange
- zest of 1 medium orange finely grated
- 1 tbsp balsamic vinegar
- 1 clove garlic peeled and crushed
- 1 tbsp clear honey
- 2 medium oranges peeled and segmented (segments halved)
- 90 g reduced-fat feta cheese roughly crumbled
- salt and back pepper to taste

Instructions

1. Preheat the oven to 200°C.
2. Place the beetroot in a medium mixing bowl with the rosemary, orange juice, orange zest, balsamic vinegar, garlic and honey. Mix well.
3. Pour the beetroot and juices into a medium ovenproof dish and roast, uncovered, in the preheated oven for 40-45 minutes, occasionally turning and basting with the juices in the dish. Take care not to let the mixture dry out. Just add a little water, if needed.
4. Roast until the beetroot is tender when tested with a sharp knife, but still retains some crunchiness. Most of the juices will have reduced, with a small amount remaining.
5. Tip the beetroot and juices into a medium mixing bowl and leave to cool. Once cooled, add the orange segments, feta and season well with salt and black pepper. Mix gently to combine and place in a serving bowl.
6. Serve as a side salad with an accompaniment of your choice.

Red Pesto Chicken Salad

PREP TIME 10 COOK TIME 15 SERVINGS 2

Ingredients

- 2 chicken breasts, approx. 130g each, sliced
- 3 tbsp red pesto
- 2 tbsp water
- 1 tbsp balsamic vinegar
- 1 tsp white granulated sweetener
- 2 cloves garlic, peeled and crushed
- 80 g lettuce
- 6 cherry tomatoes, quartered (we used red and yellow)
- 50 g cucumber, sliced into half moons
- 20 g reduced-fat feta cheese
- 11 g pine nuts
- low-calorie cooking spray
- salt and pepper, to taste

Instructions

1. In a small bowl, combine the pesto, water, balsamic vinegar, garlic and sweetener. Season with a little salt and pepper.
2. Add the chicken to a bowl and pour over half the pesto dressing. Coat the chicken, cover and pop into the fridge for a minimum of 30 minutes. If you have time, leave it longer to allow the flavours to develop further.
3. Add the pine nuts to a small frying pan and set on a low heat. Heat for 2 minutes until the pine nuts are lightly toasted and golden. Leave to one side.
4. Assemble the salad. Divide the lettuce, tomatoes and cucumber between two plates. Crumble over the feta cheese and sprinkle over the pine nuts.
5. Once the chicken has marinated, spray a frying pan with low-calorie cooking spray. Set on a medium heat and add the chicken to the pan. Cook for 10 minutes, moving the chicken round the pan to brown on all sides. Check that the chicken is cooked through, and no pinkness remains.
6. Add the chicken to the top of the salad, drizzle over the remaining dressing and serve.

Salmon and Zingy Salad

PREP TIME 12 COOK TIME 8 SERVINGS 4

Ingredients

For the salmon
- 4 boneless salmon fillets, approx. 120g each
- ¼ tsp paprika
- ¼ tsp garlic powder
- ¼ tsp onion granules
- ¼ tsp dried oregano
- ¼ tsp dried basil
- ¼ tsp dried thyme
- ¼ tsp salt
- ¼ tsp pepper
- low-calorie cooking spray

For the salad
- 1 carrot, peeled and grated or shredded using a julienne peeler
- 1 avocado, stone removed and flesh diced
- 1 red chilli, deseeded and finely diced
- 3 spring onions, finely sliced
- 25 g reduced-fat feta cheese, crumbled
- 140 g tinned sweetcorn, drained
- 25 g fresh coriander, roughly chopped
- 2 tbsp lime juice

Instructions

1. To a small bowl add the paprika, garlic powder, onion granules, thyme, basil, oregano and salt and pepper. Stir to combine.
2. Spray the pink side of the salmon fillets and coat with the spice mix.
3. Spray a large frying pan with low-calorie cooking spray and set on a medium heat. Heat for one minute.
4. Add the salmon fillets pink side down into the pan. Cook for 3 minutes and then flip over to be skin side down. Cook for a further 3 minutes. Depending on the thickness of your salmon fillets, they may need a little longer to cook through.
5. While the salmon is cooking, make the salad. Add the carrot, avocado, chilli, spring onion, sweetcorn, coriander and feta cheese to a mixing bowl. Drizzle over the lime juice and toss to coat.
6. When the salmon is cooked, serve with the salad and an extra lime wedge if you'd like!

Chicken and Bacon Caesar Salad

PREP TIME 5   COOK TIME 15   SERVINGS 4

Ingredients

- 2 skinless chicken breasts (approx. 150g/5oz each)
- 4 bacon medallions
- 300 g cos lettuce sliced
- 8 cherry tomatoes quartered
- 15 g Parmesan shavings
- 1 tsp garlic granules
- 1/4 tsp black pepper
- 1/4 tsp salt
- low calorie cooking spray

Instructions

1. Spray a frying pan with low calorie cooking spray and set on a medium heat.
2. Add the garlic granules, salt and black pepper to a small plate and mix together.
3. Take the chicken breasts and slice them in half lengthways to make 4 thin pieces. Dip the chicken breast pieces onto the plate and rub until they have a light coating.
4. Add the chicken to the pan and cook for 5 minutes on each side, until the chicken is cooked through, shows no signs of pinkness and the outside is golden and slightly crispy. Set the chicken to one side.
5. Add the bacon medallions to the pan and cook for 4 – 5 minutes or until crispy. Set aside to cool slightly.
6. In a small bowl, combine the dressing ingredients and stir until smooth.
7. Once the chicken and bacon have cooled, slice them up.
8. Assemble the salad by arranging the lettuce into a layer on the plate, add the cherry tomatoes and sprinkle with the Parmesan.
9. Add the chicken and bacon on top of the lettuce and drizzle with the dressing.

Chicken Pesto Salad

PREP TIME 5 **COOK TIME** 10 **SERVINGS** 2

Ingredients

- 2 chicken breasts, approx.130g each sliced
- 3 tbsp green pesto
- juice of 1 lemon
- 2 garlic cloves, peeled and crushed
- 1 tbsp water
- 80 g lettuce
- 5 cherry tomatoes, quartered
- 4 radishes, finely sliced
- 50 g cucumber, sliced into half moons
- 20 g reduced fat feta cheese
- 11 g pine nuts
- low-calorie cooking spray
- salt and pepper, to taste

Instructions

1. In a small bowl, combine the pesto, lemon juice, garlic, water and season with a little salt and pepper.
2. Add the chicken to a bowl and pour over half the dressing. Coat the chicken, cover and pop into the fridge for 30 minutes.
3. Add the pine nuts to a small frying pan and set on a low heat. Heat for 2 minutes until the pine nuts are lightly toasted and golden. Leave to one side.
4. Assemble the salad. Divide the lettuce, tomatoes, radish and cucumber between two plates. Crumble over the feta cheese and sprinkle over the pine nuts.
5. Once the chicken has marinated, spray a frying pan with low-calorie cooking spray. Set on a medium heat add the chicken to the pan. Cook for 10 minutes, moving the chicken round the pan to brown on all sides. Check that the chicken is cooked through, and no pinkness remains.
6. Add the chicken to the top of the salad, drizzle over the remaining dressing and serve.

Halloumi Fries Salad

PREP TIME 20 | **COOK TIME** 20 | **SERVINGS** 2

Ingredients

- For the halloumi fries
- 200 g reduced fat halloumi cheese, drained and cut into 1cm wide fries
- 25 g panko breadcrumbs
- 30 g fat free natural yoghurt
- For the salad
- 40 g rocket leaves
- 1 medium orange, peeled, segmented and cut into small chunks
- 100 g cooked fresh beetroot, cut into 1cm cubes
- 80 g cucumber, cut into 1cm cubes
- 4 tsp pomegranate seeds
- 60 g fat free natural yoghurt
- 2 tbsp reduced sugar sweet chilli sauce
- 2 g fresh mint leaves, stalks removed and roughly chopped
- salt and black pepper, to taste
- low-calorie cooking spray

Instructions

1. Preheat the oven to 200°C. Line a baking tray with foil and spray with low-calorie cooking spray. Make sure to grease the foil thoroughly.
2. Pour the yoghurt onto a small plate and sprinkle the panko breadcrumbs on another small plate.
3. Dip the halloumi pieces in the yoghurt, turning until well-coated. Dip into the breadcrumbs to coat all over, pressing the breadcrumbs on lightly.
4. Place the breadcrumbed halloumi on the prepared baking tray and spray with low-calorie spray. Pop in the preheated oven for 15-20 minutes until crisp and golden. Remove from the oven and set aside.
5. While the halloumi fries are baking, make the salad. Divide the rocket between two plates, leaving a space in the middle for the halloumi fries. Divide the orange chunks, beetroot and cucumber between the two plates and sprinkle over pomegranate seeds.
6. Place the fries in the middle of each plate. You can serve the halloumi fries hot or cold, depending on what you fancy! Season to taste with salt and black pepper but bear in mind that halloumi is already fairly salty.
7. Drizzle the yoghurt and sweet chilli sauce over the halloumi fries and sprinkle with the chopped mint leaves. Serve at once.

Greek-Style Pasta Salad

PREP TIME 15 COOK TIME 10 SERVINGS 2

Ingredients

For the salad
- 100 g small pasta shapes, eg. fusilli, penne or conchiglie
- 150 g cherry tomatoes, halved
- 75 g cucumber, sliced into half moon shapes
- ½ a red onion, peeled and finely sliced
- 10 black olives, halved
- a couple of handfuls of mixed salad leaves
- 50 g reduced fat feta or Greek salad cheese

For the dressing
- 100 g fat free Greek yoghurt
- 50 g reduced fat feta or Greek salad cheese
- juice of half a lemon
- ½ tsp garlic granules
- 2 sprigs of oregano, leaves removed from stalks
- pinch of black pepper

Instructions

1. Cook the pasta according to packet instructions (usually for 9-12 minutes in a pan of boiling salted water). Drain, rinse under cold water and transfer to a large mixing bowl.
2. While the pasta cooks, place the ingredients for the dressing in a blender and blitz to a smooth dressing.
3. Mix together the pasta, tomatoes, cucumber, onions and olives.
4. Place the salad leaves on 2 plates, divide the pasta mix between them, and crumble on the feta.
5. Drizzle over the yoghurt dressing and serve.

Tuna Niçoise Pasta Salad

PREP TIME 20 **COOK TIME** 20 **SERVINGS** 2

Ingredients

- 180g tin tuna in spring water or brine drained
- 75 g dried pasta twists
- 75 g fine green beans trimmed and cut in half
- 10 cherry tomatoes halved
- ½ red onion peeled and sliced
- 10 pitted olives
- 50 g mixed salad leaves
- 2 eggs

For the dressing

- 75 g fat free yoghurt
- 1 tsp Dijon mustard
- ¼ tsp dried dill
- pinch garlic granules
- 1 lemon juice only
- ½ tsp honey
- salt and freshly ground black pepper

Instructions

1. Boil the eggs for 8 minutes, then plunge into cold water to cool. Peel and cut in half.
2. While the eggs are cooling, cook the pasta for 9-12 minutes or according to packet instructions. Cool under some cold water and drain.
3. While the pasta is cooking, cook the green beans in a pan of boiling salted water. We cooked them for 5 minutes, so they still had some "bite" but cook them a little longer if you prefer. Plunge into cold water to cool quickly and drain well.
4. Whisk together the dressing ingredients, and season with the salt and pepper, according to taste.
5. Divide the salad leaves onto 2 plates, arrange the remaining salad ingredients on top, and serve drizzled with the dressing.

Thai-Style Chicken Salad

PREP TIME 5   **COOK TIME** 15   **SERVINGS** 4

Ingredients

- 280 g cooked chicken breast cut into strips
- ½ small white cabbage cored and finely shredded
- 1 large carrot peeled and cut into thin strips
- 450 g fresh pineapple peeled and cut into chunks
- 6 spring onions trimmed and sliced thinly
- 1 green pepper deseeded and cut into strips
- 1 red chilli deseeded and sliced thinly
- 10 g fresh coriander chopped

For the dressing

- 1 clove garlic peeled and minced
- 2 tbsp white wine vinegar
- 2 tbsp soy sauce
- 2 tbsp granulated sweetener
- 1 tbsp lime juice
- ½ tbsp fish sauce
- 4 tbsp peanut butter powder
- 4 tbsp water mixed with peanut butter powder

Instructions

1. In a small bowl add all the salad dressing ingredients and mix well.
2. On your serving plate, arrange the cabbage, carrot, pineapple, pepper, and spring onion. Top with the cooked chicken, red chilli and chopped coriander.
3. Serve with the salad dressing on the side.

Lunch & Dinner

Beef & Onion Pasties

PREP TIME 10 **COOK TIME** 1hour 25 **SERVINGS** 4

Ingredients

- 4 Weight Watchers Wraps
- 400 g ox cheek or stewing beef
- 1 white onion
- 1 red onion sliced
- 1 tbsp Worcestershire sauce
- 750 ml boiling water
- 1 tsp gravy browning
- 1 tsp onion granules
- 1 tsp garlic granules
- 1 beef stock cube
- 1 beef stock pot
- 1 egg
- 1 tsp xanthan gum

Instructions

1. Cut the ox cheeks into 2cm diced pieces and roughly dice the white onion.
2. Using the Sauté function on the Instant Pot, spray the bowl with low calorie cooking spray and brown the meat and onions for around 5 minutes.
3. Season the meat and onions with salt and pepper, add enough water (around 750ml/3 cups - you may need more, but this will be used for the gravy to serve with!) to just cover the meat and bring to the boil continuing to use the Sauté function.
4. Once the liquid is boiling, crumble in the beef stock cube and stir. Add the beef stock pot, gravy browning, Worcestershire sauce, garlic granules and onion granules and mix well.
5. Place the lid onto the Instant Pot, ensure the valve is closed. Press the "Manual" button and set the time to 60 minutes.
6. When the Instant Pot has finished cooking, quick release the pressure. Preheat the oven to 170ºC.
7. Take the lid off the Instant Pot and turn on the Sauté function. Add in the Xanthan Gum and stir very well until the gravy and beef have thickened. You may need more Xanthan Gum depending on how much liquid you used.
8. Beat the egg. Add a few spoons of meat onto on half of a wrap, and top with some sliced red onion - it's important not to over fill the pasties or they won't seal and may leak when cooking. Brush some beaten egg around the edge of the wrap and fold the wrap over. Press the edge down firmly with a fork and brush the top with the beaten egg.
9. Place on a baking tray and bake for 20 minutes until golden. Serve with your choice of accompaniment and the left over gravy!

Baked Garlic Salmon

PREP TIME 10 COOK TIME 25 SERVINGS 2

Ingredients

- 2 salmon fillets approx 150g per fillet
- 160 g tenderstem broccoli
- 1 lemon juiced
- 2 slices lemon
- 1 tbsp reduced fat spread
- 2 cloves garlic peeled and minced
- 10 g fresh parsley chopped
- 1 tbsp water
- salt and pepper to taste

Instructions

1. Pre-heat the oven to 200°C.
2. Place the broccoli in the centre of 1 piece of tin foil.
3. In a mixing bowl add the reduced fat spread, garlic, parsley, lemon juice and a pinch of salt and pepper. Mix well.
4. Spread the garlic mix over the salmon fillets and place on top of the broccoli. Top with 2 slices of lemon and add the water.
5. Place the second sheet of tin foil over the first and roll each side up to make a parcel.
6. Place the parcel onto the baking tray and place in the oven. Cook for 20-25 minutes until salmon is cooked and broccoli is tender.
7. Serve along with some of the cooked broccoli.

Pork Fillet

PREP TIME 10 **COOK TIME** 30 **SERVINGS** 4

Ingredients

- 400 g pork fillet all visible fat removed
- 3 tbsp brown granulated sweetener
- 3 tbsp balsamic vinegar
- 2 cm piece fresh ginger peeled and minced
- 2 cloves of garlic peeled and minced
- 1 red chilli deseeded and finely chopped
- 2 limes juiced
- 1 tsp cumin
- 1 tsp paprika
- 1/2 tsp oregano
- 1/2 tsp onion salt
- 1/2 tsp cayenne pepper
- 1/2 tsp salt
- 1/2 tsp freshly ground black pepper
- 10 g fresh coriander chopped
- 1 lime cut into wedges
- low calorie cooking spray

Instructions

1. Pre-heat oven to 200°C.
2. In a mixing bowl, add the brown granulated sweetener, balsamic vinegar, lime juice, ginger, garlic, and fresh chilli. Mix.
3. Add the cumin, paprika, oregano, onion salt, cayenne pepper, coriander, and the salt and pepper. Mix well.
4. Place the pork into the marinade and leave for 15-20 minutes.
5. Spray a lidded, ovenproof frying pan with low calorie cooking spray and set on a medium heat. Add the pork, reserving most of the marinade in the mixing bowl.
6. Cook the pork for 5 minutes sealing on all sides, then place into the oven with the rest of the marinade. Cover with the lid.
7. Cook for 15 minutes, then remove the lid and cook for a further 5 minutes.
8. Remove the pork from the pan and let it rest for 5 minutes before serving. Serve with some of the cooked marinade drizzled over the top and garnish with the wedges of lime.

Herb Crusted Cod

PREP TIME 15 **COOK TIME** 30 **SERVINGS** 4

Ingredients

- 4 skinless, boneless cod fillets around 170g each
- 4 tbsp low fat cream cheese

For the herb crust

- 50 g wholemeal bread
- 20 g Parmesan cheese finely grated
- 1/4 tsp mustard powder
- 1 clove of garlic finely chopped
- 1 lemon zested
- 5 g chives chopped
- 5 g curly parsley chopped
- salt and pepper to taste
- low calorie cooking spray
- extra chopped parsley to garnish optional

Instructions

1. Pre-heat the oven to 180°C. Grease an ovenproof dish with low calorie cooking spray.
2. Make the bread into breadcrumbs using a food processor or a coarse grater.
3. Place all the herb crust ingredients together in a mixing bowl and mix well.
4. Place the fish into the ovenproof dish and spread the cream cheese over the top of each piece. Season well with salt and pepper.
5. Spoon the herb crust mixture over each piece of fish, pressing it down lightly.
6. Place uncovered in the oven for 25 - 30 minutes, until the fish is cooked through. The fish should flake in the middle when it is cooked.
7. Sprinkle with chopped parsley and serve.

Salmon Spaghetti Carbonara

PREP TIME 5 **COOK TIME** 10 **SERVINGS** 4

Ingredients

- 240 g dried spaghetti
- 180 g hot smoked salmon
- 250 ml pasta water keep back before draining the pasta
- 100 g frozen peas
- 10 g parmesan finely grated
- 3 eggs
- 1 tbsp fresh chives or dried chives
- 1 tsp garlic granules
- salt and pepper
- low calorie cooking spray

Instructions

1. Cook the spag according to the instructions on the packet. In the last 4 minutes of cooking time, add the frozen peas into the spaghetti to cook through.
2. Beat the eggs in a bowl with the finely grated parmesan, chives, garlic powder, salt and pepper.
3. Drain the spaghetti and peas, but keep 250mls/1 cup of the pasta water back – you'll use this later. Keep the pasta and peas in the colander.
4. Using the pan which you cooked the spaghetti and peas in, pop back on the heat and spray with low calorie cooking spray. Flake the hot smoked salmon fillets into the pan and heat through for a few minutes.
5. Return the spaghetti and peas back to the saucepan with the salmon. Turn off the hob and remove the pan from the heat. Add the beaten egg mix, along with the pasta water and stir thoroughly, ensuring all the spaghetti is coated in the egg – this should take a couple of minutes.
6. Serve immediately and top with a little sprinkle of parmesan if required!

Tricky Mac and Cheese

PREP TIME 10 **COOK TIME** 20 **SERVINGS** 6

Ingredients

- 400 g cauliflower broken into florets
- 150 g light spreadable cheese like Primula Light or GoGo
- 1/2 tsp onion granules
- 1/2 tsp garlic granules
- 1/2 tsp mustard powder
- 200 g dried macaroni or other dried pasta
- 2 courgettes peeled and cut into 1cm cubes
- 80 g reduced fat cheddar finely grated
- low calorie cooking spray
- salt and pepper to taste
- 1 chopped spring onion to serve optional

Instructions

For the sauce

1. Add the cauliflower to a pan of boiling water and cook for 10 minutes until soft.
2. Once the cauliflower is cooked, drain the water and add to a blender with the spreadable cheese, onion granules, garlic and mustard (you could also place in a separate bowl and use a hand blender). Blend until smooth and set aside.

For the pasta

1. While the cauliflower is cooking, add the pasta to another pan of boiling water and cook for 10 minutes or until tender.
2. Add the courgette to the empty pan that the cauliflower was cooked in and spritz with low calorie cooking spray. Gently sauté over a medium heat for 5 minutes until softened and cooked through. It should be as soft as the cooked pasta.
3. Pour the sauce into the pan with the courgette, along with the drained pasta and a few tablespoons of the pasta water. Stir to combine and season with salt and pepper to taste.
4. You can serve the dish like this, or make it extra cheesy by adding to an ovenproof dish and topping with the grated cheddar. Place under the grill for 5 minutes until the top is bubbling and golden and serve with an optional sprinkle of spring onion.

Lemon Chicken

PREP TIME 5 **COOK TIME** 35 **SERVINGS** 4

Ingredients

- 4 medium chicken breasts approx 150g each
- 1 small onion finely chopped
- 1 chicken stock cube
- 300 ml boiling water
- ½ lemon juice only
- 75 g low fat cream cheese
- 50 g spinach
- black pepper
- low calorie cooking spray

Instructions

1. Spray the frying pan with low calorie cooking spray and place over a medium heat.
2. When the pan is hot, place the chicken breasts in and cook for 2 minutes each side to seal and colour. Remove to a plate and place to one side.
3. Give the pan another spray with low calorie cooking spray then add the onions and sauté for 5 minutes until soft.
4. Add the stock cube to the boiling water and pour into the pan along with the lemon juice and bring to a simmer.
5. Stir in the low fat cream cheese, then return the chicken to the pan.
6. Allow to simmer for 10-15 minutes, stirring occasionally until the chicken is cooked through.
7. The sauce should have reduced and thickened slightly, but if it is too runny turn up the heat and allow to bubble until you reach the consistency of single cream.
8. Stir in the spinach and cook for a couple more minutes until it has wilted.
9. Season with a little freshly ground black pepper and serve with your choice of accompaniment.

French Dip-Style Sandwiches

PREP TIME 20 COOK TIME 50 SERVINGS 4

Ingredients

- 500 g beef, all visible fat removed cut into chunks
- 1 medium onion peeled and roughly sliced
- 4 gluten free rolls sliced in half
- 80 g reduced fat Cheddar cheese grated
- 400 ml diet coke
- 100 ml balsamic vinegar
- 2 tbsp Worcestershire sauce
- 2 tbsp garlic granules
- 2 tbsp onion granules
- 1 tbsp mustard powder
- 1 beef stock cube
- low calorie cooking spray

Instructions

Instant Pot/Pressure Cooker

1. Add the beef, onions, garlic, onion granules, Worcestershire sauce, stock cube, diet coke, balsamic vinegar and mustard powder to the Instant Pot.
2. Lock the lid onto the pot, make sure the release valve is turned to the 'sealed' position and press 'Pressure Cook'. The pressure should be set to normal and you will need to set the time to 50 minutes.
3. When the Instant Pot beeps that is is finished, move the release valve to quick release (watch your face and hands, there will be hot steam!).
4. When the pressure is fully released take the lid off the pot and carefully remove the pieces of beef. Place them into a separate bowl and shred the meat with two forks. Place some foil over it to keep it warm.
5. Take your hand blender and whizz up the onions and liquid left in the Instant Pot. If you like your gravy thicker you can switch your Instant Pot to 'Saute' and reduce it down further.
6. Now you are ready to assemble the sandwiches. Divide the the beef and cheese between the four rolls. You can put the rolls under a hot grill for a minute to melt the cheese if you want - just make sure not to burn the bread!
7. Pour the gravy into ramekins and serve with the warm sandwiches.

Bang Bang Noodles

PREP TIME 15 **COOK TIME** 15 **SERVINGS** 2

Ingredients

- 2 nests of dried egg noodles
- 90 g reduced fat halloumi cut into 2.5cm slices
- 1 courgette julienned
- 1 carrot julienned
- 75 g baby corn cut into slices
- 2 cloves of garlic crushed
- 1 chilli deseeded and finely chopped
- pinch of chilli flakes more or less according to taste
- 3 tbsp light soy sauce
- 3 tbsp rice vinegar
- 1 tbsp tomato puree
- 2 tsp honey
- juice of 1/2 a lime
- handful of fresh coriander chopped
- low calorie cooking spray
- 2 spring onions finely sliced

Instructions

1. Place the potato in a medium saucepan of water and boil for 20 minutes or until tender. Drain well and return to the saucepan.
2. Mash the potato with the milk. Add 2 tbsp of the fresh coriander and season well with salt and pepper. Stir to combine.
3. Spray a medium saucepan with low calorie cooking spray and place on a medium heat. Fry the onions for 15 minutes, stirring occasionally, or until softened and golden brown.
4. Add the chicken, ginger, garlic, and curry powder, and fry for 4 - 5 minutes to seal the chicken on all sides.
5. Add the coconut milk, stir and simmer over a low heat, uncovered, for 15 minutes.
6. Pre-heat the oven to 180°C fan.
7. Add the almonds and simmer over a low heat for a further 15 minutes, stirring occasionally. The sauce should have thickened slightly, if not cook a little longer. Stir in the remaining 1 tbsp coriander.
8. Place the chicken Korma mixture in a 27 x 18 cm ovenproof dish and spread out.
9. Spread the potato over the top using a fork and place on a baking tray.
10. Place in the preheated oven for 20 - 25 minutes or until golden brown.
11. Remove from the oven and serve.

Slow Cooker
1. Spray a frying pan with low calorie cooking spray and set on a medium heat. Add the beef and brown on all sides.
2. Once the beef is cooked, remove it from the pan and set aside. Now add the sliced onions with a little water and soften them over a low heat for a few minutes.
3. Add the onions, beef, garlic, onion granules, Worcestershire sauce, stock cube, diet coke, balsamic vinegar and mustard powder to the slow cooker.
4. Set the slow cooker to high and place the lid on. Cook for around 6 hours.
5. When the slow cooking is completed carefully remove the pieces of beef. Place them into a separate bowl and shred the meat with two forks. Place some foil over it to keep it warm.
6. Take your hand blender and whizz up the onions and liquid left in the slow cooker. If you like your gravy thicker you can reduce the liquid further in a saucepan on the hob.
7. Now you are ready to assemble the sandwiches. Divide the the beef and cheese between the four rolls. You can put the rolls under a hot grill for a minute to melt the cheese if you want - just make sure not to burn the bread!
8. Pour the gravy into ramekins and serve with the warm sandwiches.

Rigatoni Pizza Pie

PREP TIME 25 **COOK TIME** 25 **SERVINGS** 4

Ingredients

- 400 g dried rigatoni pasta
- 100 g tomato passata
- 400 g tin of chopped tomatoes
- 4 cloves garlic
- 1 tbsp dried oregano
- 2 tbsp tomato puree
- 140 g reduced fat mozzarella
- 80 g reduced fat cheddar
- ¼ red pepper
- 2 chestnut mushrooms
- 1 tomato
- pinch granulated sweetener
- low calorie cooking spray

Instructions

1. Pre-heat the oven to 160°C. Bring a large saucepan of water to the boil.
2. Once the water is boiling, add the rigatoni pasta. Cook for 6 minutes - the pasta won't be cooked through but it will finish cooking in the oven. Set aside.
3. Finely crush the garlic into a saucepan sprayed with low calorie cooking spray and cook on a low heat for about 5 minutes, stirring frequently and being careful not to burn it.
4. Keeping the heat low, add the passata, chopped tomatoes, tomato puree and herbs. Mix well, add a pinch of sweetener and turn the heat up until it starts to bubble or "blip". Leave to reduce for 15 minutes on a moderate heat, stirring occasionally.
5. Meanwhile, finely chop the pepper and slice the mushrooms and tomato. Grate the cheddar cheese and tear the mozzarella into pieces.
6. Spray a 24cm spring form tin with low calorie cooking spray. Place the rigatoni pasta tubes upright into the tin - it's best to start at one side of the tin and work across as this keeps them more upright. Once the tin is full, squeeze as many tubes of pasta into the gaps as possible - you'll be surprised how many you can fit in!
7. Once the tin is full of the rigatoni, pour over the tomato sauce and spread over the top of the pasta. Top with the grated cheddar first, followed by the peppers, mushrooms, mozzarella and finally the tomato slices.
8. Bake in the oven for around 25 minutes until the cheese is golden. Remove from the oven and run a knife around the edge before unclipping the tin to remove the outer ring. Cut into wedges and serve with a salad!

Bacon, Onion & Potato Bake

PREP TIME 10 | **COOK TIME** 1hour15 | **SERVINGS** 4

Ingredients

- 1 kg potatoes peeled and sliced thinly
- 16 bacon medallions you can use more bacon if you wish, depending on the pack size. Some have 8 medallions, some 10 per pack
- 2 onions peeled and thinly sliced
- 1 veg stock cube or chicken stock cube made up with 200ml of boiling water
- sea salt
- freshly ground black pepper
- 40 g reduced fat cheddar grated
- low calorie cooking spray

Instructions

1. Pre-heat the oven to 180°C
2. Spread a layer of sliced onion on the bottom of an oven proof dish
3. Arrange a layer of potato slices and bacon on top of the onions, alternating a couple of slices and potato with a piece of bacon. Next add another layer of onions. Repeat until you have used up all the bacon and potatoes. You should have a couple of layers at least
4. Pour the made up stock over the top, then season with a little salt and pepper. Spray the top with a little Low calorie cooking spray, then cover with foil and seal
5. Cook for an hour, then remove the foil and check that the potato is cooked. If not cover and return it to the oven for a bit longer. When it is cooked sprinkle the cheese over the top, then return to the oven for another 10 - 15 minutes or until the cheese has melted and is golden brown

Haddock & Creamy Mustard Sauce

PREP TIME 5 **COOK TIME** 15 **SERVINGS** 4

Ingredients

- 4 large smoked haddock fillets
- 700 ml skimmed milk
- 1 tsp wholegrain mustard
- 1 tbsp cornflour
- 2 tsp mustard powder

Instructions

1. Bring the milk to a gentle simmer in the saucepan. Place the fish into the milk to poach for around 6 minutes until the fish is just cooked. The time will depend on the thickness of your fish, thicker fillets may need a couple of minutes longer.
2. Remove the fish gently from the milk and set aside. In a small bowl, add the cornflour and mix with a little drop of water to form a thin liquid. Return the milk to a low heat and whisk the cornflour liquid in.
3. Continue to whisk gently. Add the mustard powder and whole grain mustard until the sauce thickens. If you prefer a thicker or thinner sauce then add more or less cornflour - just change the Points and calories etc accordingly. Season the sauce with salt and pepper.
4. Return the fish to the sauce for 1 minute and serve with your choice of accompaniments.

Shepherd's Pie

PREP TIME 10 **COOK TIME** 55 **SERVINGS** 6

Ingredients

For the lamb base
- 350 grams lean diced lamb all visible fat removed
- 2 large carrots
- 1 large onion
- 1 large courgette
- 100 grams green beans
- 2 cloves garlic
- 100 grams frozen peas
- 1 lamb stock pot
- 2 beef stock cubes
- 2 tbsp tomato puree
- low calorie cooking spray

For the creamy mashed potatoes
- 1 kg potatoes see next page for Creamy Mashed Potatoes

Instructions

1. Preheat the oven to 180°C. Cut the diced lamb very finely, and chop the onion.
2. Spray a large saucepan with low calorie cooking spray and brown the lamb for 5-6 minutes. Slice the carrots, chop the green beans and grate the courgette, and add to the saucepan along with the onion and garlic.
3. Cook the veg for around 5 minutes until they have just started to soften.
4. Add the tomato puree, lamb stock pot and beef stock cubes. Cover with boiling water (around 900ml, depending on the size of your saucepan), mix thoroughly and pop a lid on. Cook for 25 minutes on a low heat, stirring occasionally to ensure it doesn't stick to the bottom.
5. Meanwhile, cook the Creamy Mashed Potatoes from our recipe, making double the amount! The spring onions are optional.
6. Remove the lid from the meat, add the frozen peas and leave to reduce on a high heat for around 5 minutes.
7. Pour the meat into a baking dish, top with the mashed potatoes, spray with low calorie cooking spray and place in the oven for 30 minutes until golden and crisp!

Creamy Mashed Potatoes

PREP TIME 5 COOK TIME 20 SERVINGS 2

Ingredients

- 500 g potatoes peeled and cut into chunks
- 1 tbsp fresh chives chopped - or you can use 1 or 2 finely chopped spring onions
- salt and pepper to taste

Instructions

1. Bring a pan of salted water to the boil.
2. Place the chopped potato in the pan and cook for 15 to 20 minutes or until they are tender.
3. While the potatoes are cooking finely chop the chives or spring onion.
4. Drain the cooked potato, then return to the pan. Add some salt and pepper.
5. Mash the potato, using a hand blender with a mashing attachment or a potato masher.
6. When all the lumps have gone and the potato is a nice smooth texture stir in the chives/spring onion. Check the seasoning and add a little more if necessary. Stir well and serve.

Beef with Ginger & Spring Onion

PREP TIME 15 **COOK TIME** 15 **SERVINGS** 4

Ingredients

- 500 g rump/sirloin/fillet/topside beef thinly sliced
- 2 cloves garlic finely chopped
- 2 cm ginger finely chopped
- 1 onion sliced
- 80 ml oyster sauce
- 3 tbsp soy sauce, preferably dark
- 2 tbsp rice vinegar
- 1 tsp granulated sweetener optional
- 1 red pepper
- 1 yellow pepper
- 1 green pepper
- 5 large mushrooms sliced
- 4 spring onions sliced
- 5 baby corn
- low calorie cooking spray

Instructions

1. Spray a large frying pan or wok with low calorie cooking spray and gently heat.
2. Brown the beef on both sides in small batches, just to colour the beef. DO NOT let it cook through. Set aside.
3. Deglaze the pan with 1 tbsp of rice vinegar and a bit of water. Make sure to get all the beef that is stuck to the bottom. This will give your dish real depth of flavour.
4. Spray the pan with some more low calorie cooking spray and fry the onion, garlic, ginger and mushrooms until the onion is soft.
5. Add the rice vinegar, oyster sauce, soy sauce and sweetener if using, cook until it thickens.
6. Add the beef back to the pan along with the chopped spring onions and cook for a further 5 minutes stirring often.
7. Add the peppers and baby corn, cook for a further 2-3 minutes. Serve and enjoy!

Garlic Mushroom Risotto

PREP TIME 10   **COOK TIME** 55   **SERVINGS** 3

Ingredients

- 300 g arborio rice
- 1 onion chopped
- 3 cloves garlic finely chopped
- 80 g frozen peas
- 1 tbsp Henderson's Relish or Worcestershire sauce
- 300 g mushrooms sliced
- 1.4 l vegetable stock 2 stock cubes made up with 1.4l of boiling water
- 2 tbsp white wine vinegar
- ½ lemon juice only
- 1 handful fresh parsley chopped
- 90 g Parmesan cheese finely grated, omit if vegetarian
- low calorie cooking spray

Instructions

1. Add the onions, 200g of the sliced mushrooms and the garlic to the Actifry Pan. Spray with low calorie cooking spray and add the Hendersons relish. Cook for 5 Minutes.
2. Add the rice and cook for another 3 minutes.
3. Add the stock, white wine vinegar and remaining 100g of mushrooms.
4. Cook for 45 minutes.
5. Add the peas, lemon juice, pecorino, chopped parsley and black pepper. Cook for another 3 minutes.

Fish and Chip Pie

PREP TIME 20   **COOK TIME** 55   **SERVINGS** 4

Ingredients

- 5 medium potatoes peeled
- 550 g skinless and boneless cod fillet cut into large chunks
- 250 ml semi skimmed milk
- 4 spring onions cut into slices
- 1/2 lemon zested
- 2 300g tins of mushy peas
- 2 tbsp cornflour
- 1 tbsp water
- 2 tsp malt vinegar
- salt and pepper to taste
- low calorie cooking spray

Instructions

1. Pre-heat the oven to 200ºC.
2. Cut the potatoes into 1cm wide slices, then cut the slices into 1cm wide chips and place in a bowl of cold water to rinse off the starch.
3. Tip the chips into a colander and drain away the starchy water. Place the chips on absorbent kitchen paper and pat dry.
4. Place the dry chips on a non stick baking tray and spray well with low calorie cooking spray. Place in the preheated oven for 20 minutes, turning the chips once. The chips will be slightly tender at this point but not completely cooked. Remove from the oven and set aside.
5. Place the fish in a medium frying pan with the milk, spring onion and lemon zest. Season well with salt and pepper and place over a low heat. Cover with a lid and simmer for 10 minutes, until the fish is just starting to flake. Don't stir otherwise the fish will break up.
6. Spray the ovenproof dish with a little low calorie spray and use to grease the dish.
7. Place the mushy peas in the ovenproof dish and spread out evenly.
8. Remove the frying pan from the heat, and using a large slotted spoon, remove the fish from the cooking liquid and place evenly on top of the mushy peas. Keep the cooking liquid in the frying pan as this will be used to make the sauce.
9. Mix the cornflour with the water until smooth. Tip into the cooking liquid in the frying pan and stir until evenly mixed in. Place over a low heat and simmer for 3 - 4 minutes, stirring, until slightly thickened.
10. Pour the sauce over the fish and mushy peas in the ovenproof dish.
11. Place the chips in a medium bowl and spray with low calorie cooking spray. Add the vinegar and season well with salt and pepper. Toss the chips to coat them well.
12. Place the chips evenly on top of the pie. Place on a baking tray and bake in the oven for 15 - 20 minutes. The pie should be piping hot and the chips should be tender throughout and lightly browned.
13. You can sprinkle the chips with pepper and vinegar

Hunter's Chicken

PREP TIME 10 **COOK TIME** 60 **SERVINGS** 4

Ingredients

- 4 chicken breasts, approx. 150g each
- 4 bacon medallions
- 80 g reduced-fat Cheddar, grated
- ½ onion, diced
- 2 cloves garlic, crushed
- 400 g tin chopped tomatoes
- 1 tbsp tomato puree
- ½ lemon, juiced
- 1 tbsp BBQ seasoning
- ¼ tsp smoked paprika, you can use chilli powder or normal paprika if you don't have this
- 1 tbsp balsamic vinegar
- 2 tbsp Worcestershire sauce or Henderson's relish
- 2 tbsp white wine vinegar
- 1 tbsp hot sauce
- 1 tsp mustard powder
- 1 tsp granulated sweetener

Instructions

1. Take each chicken breast, wrap a bacon medallion around the middle and secure it with a cocktail stick.
2. Set the chicken aside, then add all of the remaining ingredients into an oven-proof dish with a tight fitting lid.
3. Place the chicken on top and replace the lid. Cook for 1 hour at 180°C.
4. When the time is up check that the chicken is cooked. Remove it from the dish and set aside.
5. Blitz the sauce with a stick blender until smooth.
6. Place the cooked chicken in an ovenproof dish and remove the cocktail sticks.
7. Pour the sauce over the chicken breasts and top with cheese. Divide the cheese equally between all four chicken breasts.
8. Place under a hot grill until the cheese is melted and a nice golden colour.

Cumberland Pie

PREP TIME 10 **COOK TIME** 45 **SERVINGS** 6

Ingredients

- 750 g braising steak all visible fat removed and cut into big chunks
- 2 onions diced
- 3 medium carrots peeled and cut into big chunks
- 2 sticks celery cut into chunks
- 1 beef stock cube made up with 450ml of boiling water
- 2 Knorr Rich stock pots
- 2 tbsp tomato puree
- 1 handful fresh thyme
- 3 bay leaves
- 2 tbsp Worcestershire sauce
- 900 g potatoes
- 3 tbsp cornflour
- 120 g reduced fat cheddar grated
- sea salt
- freshly ground black pepper
- low calorie cooking spray

Instructions

In the Instant Pot

1. Make up the stock using 1 beef stock cube and 450ml / 2 cups of boiling water, then season the meat well, with sea salt and freshly ground black pepper.
2. Set the Instant Pot to Sauté and spray with a little low calorie cooking spray. Brown the meat a little at a time and set aside.
3. Add a little of the stock to the Instant Pot and stir to deglaze. When there are no bits left on the bottom of the pan, add the chopped veg and a few sprigs of thyme. Allow to cook until the veg starts to soften.
4. Stir in the tomato puree and Worcestershire sauce, then add the rest of the stock, meat and bay leaves.
5. Put the lid on the Instant Pot and set to pressure cook on Manual for 15 minutes, Natural Pressure Release (NPR).
6. While the meat is cooking, peel the potatoes and cook them until they are almost cooked, but still quite firm. You can do this in the microwave (for about 8-10 minutes) or in a pan of boiling water.
7. Allow the potatoes to cool slightly and cut them into slices about 1cm thick.
8. When the Instant Pot has finished, leave it for about 15-17 minutes to release the pressure naturally. After 15-17 minute (until the float drops) open the lid, then set back to Sauté. Stir in the stock pots.
9. Mix the cornflour with a little water, then pour it into the pot, stirring well (but be careful not to break up the meat too much!)
10. Pour the mixture into a decent sized casserole or lasagne dish. Top with the sliced potato and spray with some low calorie cooking spray.
11. Cook for 20 minutes at 200°C, then top with the grated cheese and cook for another 10 minutes until the cheese has melted and browned.

In the oven or on the stove method
1. Make up the stock using 1 beef stock cube and 450ml / 2 cups of boiling water, then season the meat well, with sea salt and freshly ground black pepper.
2. Using a pan that's suitable for the oven, brown the meat a little at a time and set aside. Then saute the onion, carrots, celery and a few sprigs of thyme.
3. When the veg has softened stir in the Worcestershire sauce and tomato puree.
4. Add the stock, beef and bay leaves. Stir, then bring to the boil. Cover with a lid and cook for 2-2½ hours in the oven at 150°C (you can do this on the stove, but keep an eye on it to make sure it doesn't boil dry.
5. While the meat is cooking, peel the potatoes and cook them until they are almost cooked, but still quite firm. You can do this in the microwave (for about 8-10 minutes) or in a pan of boiling water. Let them cool slightly then cut them into 1cm / ½ inch slices.
6. When 2-2½ hours is up, stir in the stock pots and mix the cornflour with a little water, then pour it in, stirring well.
7. Pour the mixture into a decent sized casserole or lasagne dish. Top with the sliced potato and spray with some low calorie cooking spray.
8. Cook for 20 minutes at 200°C, then top with the grated cheese and cook for another 10 minutes until the cheese has melted and browned.

Fakeaways

Nando's Peri Peri Chicken

PREP TIME 5 **COOK TIME** 40 **SERVINGS** 4

Ingredients

- 650 grams chicken thigh fillets all skin and visible fat removed
- 1 tbsp paprika
- 2 tsp garlic granules
- 1 tsp hot chilli powder
- 1 tsp onion granules
- 1 tsp granulated sweetener
- 2 tsp tomato puree
- 2 peppers
- 2 small red onions
- 1 lemon
- ¼ tsp xanthan gum
- low calorie cooking spray

Instructions

1. Preheat the oven to 180°C. Remove any fat or skin from the chicken and place in a baking dish.
2. Chop the onions and peppers into large chunks and place in the baking dish. Spray with low calorie cooking spray.
3. Sprinkle over all the spices, xanthan gum and tomato purée all over the chicken and vegetable, and add the lemon juice. Mix to combine fully.
4. Place in the oven and cook for 40 minutes until the chicken is browned and cooked through. You may need to add a couple of tablespoons of water to the dish to make some extra sauce – it really depends on how much liquid comes out of the vegetables and chicken during the cooking process.
5. Serve with rice and a wedge of lemon!

Chicken Tikka Kebabs

PREP TIME 20   **COOK TIME** 20   **SERVINGS** 4

Ingredients

Tikka Seasoning Mix
- 3 tsp Paprika
- 2 tsp Ground Coriander
- 2 tsp Ground Cumin
- 2 tsp Garam Masala
- 1.5 tsp Turmeric
- 1 tsp Ground Ginger
- 1 tsp Garlic Powder
- 1 tsp Salt
- 1/4 tsp Black Pepper
- 1/4 tsp Cayenne Pepper

Chicken Tikka
- 2 tbsp Tikka Seasoning Mix
- 4 large Chicken Breasts cut into chunks
- 3 tbsp 0% Fat Yoghurt
- juice of 1 Lemon
- 2 drops Red Food Colouring optional
- Low Calorie Cooking Spray

Instructions

Tikka seasoning mix
1. Mix all of the ingredients together & place in a glass jar. Preferably one with a tight lid

Chicken Tikka Kebabs
1. Cut the chicken breasts into chunks about the size and thickness of a chicken nugget. Place into a non-reactive bowl
2. Add the lemon juice and mix well so all of the pieces are coated
3. Add 2 tbsp of the Tikka Seasoning Mix and mix well. Then add the yoghurt (and food colouring if you're using it) and mix well. Cover with clingfilm and place in the fridge for at least 1 hour
4. Pre-heat an oven to 200°C
5. Thread the chicken onto the bamboo skewers. Spray the chicken skewers with low calorie cooking spray
6. Heat a cast iron griddle pan (or mist a frying pan with Frylight & heat, if you don't have one). When the pan is very hot, add the chicken, and cook on each side until the chicken colours
7. Once coloured on all sides, place the chicken in the oven for 5-10 minutes until the chicken is cooked through

Chicken Shawarma

PREP TIME 5 COOK TIME 10 SERVINGS 2

Ingredients

For the wraps
- 1 large chicken breast cut into strips
- 1 lemon juice only
- 2 cloves garlic crushed
- 1 tsp paprika
- 1 tsp ground cumin
- 1 tsp all spice
- ½ tsp ground coriander
- 1 pinch chilli flakes you can use as much or as little as you like depending on how spicy you like it
- 1 pinch cinnamon
- 1 tsp salt
- 2 Weight Watchers Low Fat White Wraps
- low calorie cooking spray
- 8 cherry tomatoes or 1 large tomato - chopped
- ½ red onion thinly sliced
- 2 handfuls iceberg lettuce finely shredded
- 3 tbsp pickled cabbage

For the Yoghurt Dressing
- 2 cloves garlic
- 1 pinch salt
- 1 squeeze lemon juice
- 6 tbsp fat free natural yoghurt

Instructions

To make the wraps
1. Put the chicken strips in a large bowl, then add all the remaining ingredients (apart from the wraps!)
2. Spray with low calorie cooking spray, then mix well so that all the chicken pieces are coated. Cover and place in the fridge.
3. Preheat the Tefal OptiGrill - Turn the grill on, select the chicken programme and then press OK.
4. When the light turns blue and the machine beeps, this indicates that it is ready to cook.
5. Place the chicken strips on the OptiGrill and close the lid.
6. The indicator light will go through a series of colour changes to show the different degrees of cooking. When the indicator turns red and beeps, the chicken is ready.
7. Remove the chicken from the grill using tongs.
8. To assemble the shawarma, arrange a handful of iceberg lettuce on each wrap and divide the pickled cabbage between the two. Place the chicken on the pickled cabbage, then top with chopped tomatoes and onions.
9. Drizzle over some of the yoghurt dressing, roll up the wraps, cut each one in half and serve.

To make the yoghurt dressing
1. Mix all the ingredients together well

Lamb Rogan Josh

PREP TIME 10 | COOK TIME 40 | SERVINGS 4

Ingredients

For the Curry Paste
- 2 large onions
- 2 cloves garlic minced
- 2 cm piece of ginger minced
- 1 chilli chopped
- 2 tbsp paprika
- 1½ tbsp garam masala
- 1 tbsp ground cumin
- 1 tbsp ground coriander
- 2 tsp turmeric
- 1 tsp smoked paprika
- 3 tbsp tomato puree
- 80 g red pepper from a jar in brine!
- pinch salt and pepper

For the Curry
- 500 g lean diced lamb
- 2 tbsp fat free yogurt to marinade the lamb
- 2 tbsp curry paste to marinade the lamb
- 1 tin chopped tomatoes
- 1 beef stock cube
- 4 tbsp curry paste to make the curry
- 2 tbsp fat free yogurt to finish the curry
- 2 large peppers sliced
- 200 g butternut squash diced
- 200 g cauliflower
- 30 g fresh coriander roughly chopped
- 125 ml water
- low calorie cooking spray

Instructions

To Make The Paste
1. Spray a frying pan with low calorie cooking spray, and fry the onion, ginger and chilli until brown.
2. Place the fried onions, garlic and chilli into a food processor along with all of the Curry Paste ingredients
3. Blitz until smooth.
4. Place the rogan josh curry paste in a sterilised jar. The mix will last a few days. You can also freeze it into ice cube trays.

To Make The Curry
1. Place the lamb into a non reactive bowl along with 2 tbsp of the curry paste. Add 2 tbsp of fat free yogurt (natural or Greek) and some salt and pepper.
2. Mix well, then cover with cling film and place in the fridge for at least an hour.
3. Spray a large frying pan/wok with low calorie cooking spray.
4. Fry off 4 tbsp of the rogan josh curry paste for a few minutes until it begins to stick to the bottom of the pan
5. Add the tinned tomatoes, and stock cube (just crumble it in). Fry until the mixture starts to boil
6. Add the marinated lamb, vegetables and the water to the pan. Bring to a boil, then place a lid on the pan and simmer for 30 minutes.
7. Remove from the heat, and add 2 tbsp of fat free yogurt, and a small bunch of roughly chopped coriander – stir well. Then serve!

Sausage Rolls

PREP TIME 10   **COOK TIME** 30   **SERVINGS** 3

Ingredients

- 400 g 5% pork mince
- ½ onion finely chopped
- ½ tsp thyme freshly chopped or dried
- ½ tsp sage freshly chopped or dried
- 1 tsp fresh parsley chopped
- 2 eggs reserve one for glazing
- 3 Weight Watchers wraps
- 1 tsp sea salt
- ½ tsp freshly ground black pepper
- 1 dash Worcestershire sauce
- ½ tsp mustard powder
- low calorie cooking spray

Instructions

1. Pre-heat the oven to 200°C
2. Place the mince in a large bowl
3. Add all the rest of the ingredients, (apart from 1 egg) and mix thoroughly
4. Spray a baking tray with some low calorie cooking spray
5. Divide the sausage meat into 6 equal sausage shapes
6. Place the sausages on the baking tray and cook for 15 minutes
7. Remove them from the oven and leave them to cool so they are cool enough to handle
8. Lay a Weight Watchers wrap flat and brush all over the top with the beaten egg
9. Place 2 sausages at one end and roll them up tightly in the wrap
10. Cut in half. You can cut the ends off the wrap just to tidy them up a little
11. Place the 6 sausage rolls on the baking tray and brush each one with the remaining beaten egg
12. Place them on the prepared baking tray and cook for another 10 minutes, or until they are golden brown
13. Allow to cool for a few minutes before serving

Chicken Fajitas

PREP TIME 10 COOK TIME 18 SERVINGS 4

Ingredients

- 3 chicken breasts visible skin and fat removed, sliced into strips
- 2 peppers sliced
- 1 onion sliced
- 1 tbsp ground cumin
- 1 tbsp ground coriander
- 1 tsp garlic salt
- 1 tsp chilli powder
- 1 tsp chilli flakes
- 2 tbsp tomato puree
- 100 ml water
- low calorie cooking spray

Instructions

1. Spray a frying pan with low calorie cooking spray. Cook the chicken strips for 5 minutes.
2. Combine the spices in a pestle and mortar, or bowl, and add to the chicken with the tomato puree. Cook out for 3 minutes.
3. Add the sliced peppers and onions, and the water. Mix well and leave to cook for 10 minutes.
4. Serve with wraps or rice, and a dollop of fat free yoghurt!

Sesame Chicken Drumsticks

PREP TIME 10 COOK TIME 45 SERVINGS 12

Ingredients

- 12 medium chicken drumsticks skinned
- 2 tbsp clear honey
- 2 tbsp dark soy sauce
- 2 tbsp balsamic vinegar
- 1 tbsp tomato puree
- 1 clove garlic crushed
- 3cm piece root ginger peeled and finely grated
- 5 spring onions chopped
- 1 tsp sesame seeds toasted

Instructions

1. Preheat oven to 190°.
2. In a small bowl mix together the honey, soy sauce, balsamic vinegar, tomato puree, garlic, ginger and 4 of the spring onions, reserving one chopped spring onion for garnish.
3. Using a small sharp knife, cut 3 diagonal slits into each drumstick and place in a shallow ovenproof dish.
4. Pour the marinade over and place into a preheated oven, uncovered, for 35-45 minutes, turning once halfway through. Cook until the marinade has reduced and the chicken is thoroughly cooked through.
5. Sprinkle the remaining spring onion and sesame seeds over the drumsticks and serve.

Mushroom and Spinach Lasagne

PREP TIME 30　　**COOK TIME** 45　　**SERVINGS** 4

Ingredients

- 6 sheets no precook wholewheat lasagne sheets
- 1 medium onion chopped
- 1 medium red pepper diced
- 1 medium egg beaten
- 430 g medium flat mushrooms sliced
- 400 g tinned chopped tomatoes drained
- 460 g ricotta cheese
- 260 g fresh spinach leaves rinsed and drained
- 1 clove garlic crushed
- 25 g Parmesan cheese grated
- 40 g 30% less fat Cheddar cheese grated
- 4 tbsp skimmed milk
- 2 tbsp Henderson's Relish
- 1 tbsp tomato puree
- 1 tsp dried oregano
- low calorie cooking spray
- salt and pepper to taste

Instructions

1. Pre-heat oven to 180°C.
2. Place a medium frying pan on a medium heat and spray with low calorie cooking spray. Add the onion and fry for 5 minutes until softened.
3. Add the red pepper, garlic and mushrooms and fry for 15 minutes, uncovered.
4. Add the drained chopped tomatoes, oregano, Henderson's Relish and tomato puree, stirring well. Season to taste and set aside.
5. Place the rinsed spinach in a saucepan and cook uncovered over a low heat, stirring occasionally for 3 - 4 minutes until wilted. Place the spinach in a sieve over a bowl and squeeze out excess liquid by pressing with a wooden spoon.
6. In a medium bowl, mix the ricotta, egg, milk, Parmesan and season with salt and pepper.
7. Place half of the mushroom mixture in the bottom of a 27 x 18 cm (1.5 litre) ovenproof dish and spread out evenly.
8. Place half of the spinach over the mushroom mixture and spread out.
9. Place 3 sheets of lasagne on top of the spinach, trimming to fit if needed.
10. Place half of the ricotta mixture over the lasagne sheets and spread to cover.
11. Place the remaining mushroom mixture over the ricotta layer and spread out.
12. Place the remaining spinach on top of the mushroom mixture and spread out.
13. Place 3 sheets of lasagne on top of the spinach, trimming to fit if needed.
14. Finish with a top layer of the remaining ricotta mixture, spreading to cover the lasagne. Sprinkle with grated Cheddar cheese.
15. Place on a baking tray and place in the preheated oven for 45 - 50 minutes, until the lasagne is tender when tested with a knife and the top is golden.

Chicken Jalfrezi

PREP TIME 5   **COOK TIME** 20   **SERVINGS** 6

Ingredients

For the chicken marinade
- 600 g chicken breast diced
- 1 tsp ground cumin
- 1 tsp turmeric
- 1 tsp ground coriander
- 1 tsp chilli flakes
- 1/2 tsp cumin seeds

For the sauce
- 1 onion diced
- 1 red pepper diced
- 1 green pepper diced
- 1 green chilli seeds removed and finely diced
- 50 g courgette finely diced
- 400 g can of chopped tomatoes
- 2 tbsp tomato puree
- 2 cloves of garlic crushed
- 5 cm piece of ginger finely grated
- 2 tsp garam masala
- 1 tsp ground cumin
- 1 tsp ground coriander
- 1 chicken stock cube
- 50 ml water

Instructions

For the chicken marinade
1. Add the diced chicken to a bowl and sprinkle over the marinade spices. Stir until the chicken is completely coated. Cover with cling film and pop in the fridge for 10 minutes.
2. Spray a large frying pan with low calorie cooking spray and brown the chicken until sealed on all sides.
3. Add the onions to the pan and continue to fry for 3 minutes until they begin to soften. Add the peppers and chilli and fry for a further 2 minutes.
4. Once the peppers have begun to soften, add the chopped courgette, garlic, ginger and stir until fully combined.
5. Pour in the chopped tomatoes, tomato puree and the water.
6. Crumble the stock cube into the pan and sprinkle in the coriander, cumin and garam masala give the pan a good stir.
7. Allow to bubble for 5 - 10 minutes until the vegetables are soft and the sauce is heated through. If the sauce looks a little thick then add some extra water.
8. Stir through the chopped coriander and serve.

Noodles with Chicken

PREP TIME 15 **COOK TIME** 15 **SERVINGS** 4

Ingredients

- 420 g chicken breast cut into strips
- 1 red pepper cut into strips
- 200 g tenderstem broccoli cut into florets
- 1 onion peeled and sliced
- 6 spring onions trimmed and chopped
- 3 cloves of garlic peeled and grated
- 1 large carrot peeled and cut into ribbons using a potato peeler
- 1 red chilli deseeded and chopped
- 3 tbsp oyster sauce
- 2 tbsp fish sauce
- 3 tbsp soy sauce
- 10 g Thai basil chopped
- 2 eggs lightly beaten with a fork
- 1/2 tsp chilli flakes
- 200 g egg noodles
- low calorie cooking spray
- salt and pepper to taste

Instructions

1. In a mixing bowl add the soy sauce, oyster sauce, fish sauce and chilli flakes, and mix well. Place the noodles in a saucepan of boiling salted water and cook for 6-8 minutes, then drain and rinse in cold water to stop them cooking.
2. Place a wok on a medium to high heat, spray with low calorie cooking spray and cook the chicken for 3-5 minutes until browned.
3. Push the chicken to one side and add the onion, chilli, pepper, garlic, carrot and broccoli, and cook until broccoli is tender.
4. Push all the ingredients to one side and add the beaten egg. Stir until the egg has cooked through, then add the noodles and mix well.
5. Cook the noodles for 2 minutes then add the soy sauce mix and the chopped Thai basil. Cook until the sauce has thickened slightly.
6. Season to taste with salt and pepper.
7. Sprinkle with spring onions and serve.

Chicken Korma Curry

PREP TIME 15 | **COOK TIME** 30 | **SERVINGS** 4

Ingredients

For the Korma spice mix
- 1 tsp ground coriander
- 1 tsp ground paprika
- 1 tsp turmeric
- ½ tsp ground cumin
- ¼ tsp cardamon powder or the seeds from 10 pods - pestled/bashed/whizzed
- ¼ tsp ground cinnamon
- ¼ tsp ground black pepper
- 1 pinch ground cloves
- 1 pinch dried chilli flakes

For the Korma Curry
- 3 chicken breasts diced
- 1 can chopped tomatoes 400g
- 25 g coconut flour
- 200 g fat free yoghurt
- ½ butternut squash (or pumpkin) peeled and diced
- 1 onion chopped
- 3 peppers sliced - which ever colour you like
- 2 carrots peeled and diced
- 2 garlic cloves finely chopped
- 2 cm fresh ginger finely chopped
- 1 tbsp tomato puree
- 2 chicken stock cubes
- 2 tbsp reduced fat margarine spread
- ½ tsp granulated sweetener
- 1 lime juice of
- 4 drops coconut essence
- 2 tbsp water
- low calorie cooking spray

Instructions

On the Stove

1. Place the diced butternut squash & carrot in a bowl along with 2 tbsp of water. Cover with clingfilm and microwave for 7-8 minutes until soft.
2. Meanwhile, spray a frying pan with low calorie cooking spray and gently heat. Fry the ginger, onion and garlic until the onion has browned.
3. Once browned, empty the pan into a food processor (or bowl if you have a stick blender) along with the tomato puree, chopped tomatoes, 2 chicken stock cubes, coconut flour, and the cooked carrot and butternut squash (including the water in the bowl) - blitz until smooth.
4. Spray a large pan with low calorie cooking spray and gently heat. Pour the mixture from the food processor into it along with... the lime juice, reduced fat margarine spread, the spice mix, granulated sweetener, yogurt and coconut essence. Stir Well.
5. Add the raw diced chicken. Simmer with the lid on for 20 mins making sure to stir often. You may need to add a little water depending on your desired thickness of the sauce.
6. Once the 20 minutes are up, add the sliced peppers and cook for a further 10 minutes.
7. Taste and enjoy! If you'd like it more creamy, just add a little more yogurt.

n the Slow Cooker
- Place the diced butternut squash & carrot in a bowl along with 2 tbsp of water. Cover with clingfilm and microwave for 7-8 minutes until soft.
- Meanwhile, spray a frying pan with low calorie cooking spray and gently heat. Fry the ginger, onion and garlic until the onion has browned.
- Once browned, empty the pan into a food processor (or bowl if you have a stick blender) along with the tomato puree, chopped tomatoes, 2 chicken stock cubes, coconut flour, and the cooked carrot and butternut squash (including the water in the bowl) - blitz until smooth.
- Empty the paste into the slow cooker and add all the other ingredients except the peppers. Cook for 5 to 6 hours on normal/medium.
- In the last 30 minutes add the peppers. Enjoy!

Chicken Teriyaki Kebabs

PREP TIME 10 COOK TIME 40 SERVINGS 4

Ingredients

- 600 g skinless and boneless chicken thigh fillets cut into chunks
- 2 tbsp dark soy sauce
- 1 tbsp white wine vinegar
- 2 tbsp tomato puree
- 2 tbsp granulated sweetener
- ½ tsp dried chilli flakes
- 1 tbsp fish sauce
- 2 cloves garlic peeled and finely grated
- 1 tbsp fresh ginger finely grated
- 1 lime juice and zest
- low calorie cooking spray

Instructions

1. Place all the ingredients into a bowl and mix well.
2. Cover and chill in the fridge for an hour.
3. Once marinated, thread the meat onto a skewer, spray with low calorie cooking spray and place onto a hot barbecue for 35 minutes until thoroughly cooked through. If cooking in an oven, preheat the oven to 180°C and cook for 35 - 40 minutes until cooked through.
4. Serve with savoury rice, or your choice of accompaniment!

Chicken Gyros Kebabs

PREP TIME 30   **COOK TIME** 2 hours   **SERVINGS** 4

Ingredients

- 9 chicken thighs skin & bone removed
- 200 ml fat free natural yogurt
- 1 tsp garam masala or curry powder
- 1 tsp garlic powder
- 1 tsp paprika
- 1 tsp ground cumin
- 1 pinch cinnamon
- 1 tsp salt
- 1 lemon juice only

Instructions

1. Mix all the ingredients (except the chicken) in a non reactive bowl (anything but metal!).
2. Marinade the chicken for a few hours but preferably overnight.
3. Place the chicken onto skewers and pack tightly.
4. To cook on a BBQ, cook on a direct heat until cooked, making sure to turn frequently. This should take between 1 - 1.5 hours.
5. To cook in the oven, balance on a roasting tin and cook at 180°C for 1.5-2 hours, making sure to turn the skewer a few times during cooking.

Indian-Style Fried Rice

PREP TIME 5   **COOK TIME** 15   **SERVINGS** 2

Ingredients

- 250 g cooked rice basmati or long grain
- 2 red onions chopped
- 4 baby red peppers deseeded and chopped
- 1 carrot finely diced
- 10 baby plum tomatoes finely chopped
- 1/2 tsp ground cumin
- 1/2 tsp ground coriander
- 1/2 tsp garlic powder
- 1/2 tsp paprika
- 1/2 tsp garam masala or curry powder
- 1/4 tsp ground ginger
- 1 pinch of chilli powder
- 2 -3 handfuls of fresh coriander
- low calorie cooking spray

Instructions

1. Chop the onions and peppers into thick chunks and finely dice the carrot and tomatoes.
2. Spray a good amount of low calorie cooking spray into a frying pan and place over a high heat. Once the pan is hot and the cooking spray has turned clear, add your spices.
3. Stir the spices for 10 - 20 seconds.
4. Add all of your veg to the pan. Keep an eye on it and mix regularly to stop it from sticking and burning. Cook until the vegetables have softened, but still have some bite - this should take around 10 minutes.
5. Add the cooked rice and stir again for 2 - 3 minutes until the vegetables and spices are completely incorporated into the rice.
6. At the last minute, add the chopped coriander and stir once more. Serve with some fresh lime juice over the top.

Chicken Korma Pie

PREP TIME 15　　**COOK TIME** 1h 10　　**SERVINGS** 4

Ingredients

- 650 g chicken breast diced
- 800 g potatoes peeled and cut into chunks
- 1 large onion peeled and finely chopped
- 75 ml semi-skimmed milk
- 2 cm piece of root ginger peeled and grated
- 2 cloves of garlic crushed
- 2 tbsp mild curry powder
- 400 ml tin of light coconut milk
- 3 tbsp ground almonds
- 3 tbsp fresh coriander leaves chopped
- salt and freshly ground black pepper to taste
- low calorie cooking spray

Instructions

1. Place the potato in a medium saucepan of water and boil for 20 minutes or until tender. Drain well and return to the saucepan.
2. Mash the potato with the milk. Add 2 tbsp of the fresh coriander and season well with salt and pepper. Stir to combine.
3. Spray a medium saucepan with low calorie cooking spray and place on a medium heat. Fry the onions for 15 minutes, stirring occasionally, or until softened and golden brown.
4. Add the chicken, ginger, garlic, and curry powder, and fry for 4 - 5 minutes to seal the chicken on all sides.
5. Add the coconut milk, stir and simmer over a low heat, uncovered, for 15 minutes.
6. Pre-heat the oven to 180°C fan.
7. Add the almonds and simmer over a low heat for a further 15 minutes, stirring occasionally. The sauce should have thickened slightly, if not cook a little longer. Stir in the remaining 1 tbsp coriander.
8. Place the chicken Korma mixture in a 27 x 18 cm ovenproof dish and spread out.
9. Spread the potato over the top using a fork and place on a baking tray.
10. Place in the preheated oven for 20 - 25 minutes or until golden brown.
11. Remove from the oven and serve.

Tex Mex Burgers

PREP TIME 10 **COOK TIME** 10 **SERVINGS** 4

Ingredients

- 500 grams lean 5% beef mince
- 1 small onion
- ½ tsp salt
- ½ tsp freshly ground black pepper
- 1 whole fresh chilli very finely chopped
- 1 tsp chilli powder mild or hot, depending on your taste
- 1 tsp chipotle chilli flakes
- ½ tsp garlic salt
- ½ tsp dried oregano
- ½ tsp ground cumin
- low calorie cooking spray

Instructions

1. Chop the onion finely and add to a large bowl.
2. Add all of the spices, salt, herbs and fresh chilli to the bowl and mix with the onions.
3. Add the minced beef and mix well. Make sure you squeeze the mince up with your hands as this will improve the texture of your burger. Continue to do this for a few minutes.
4. Heat a large frying pan on a medium heat. Split the burger mix into 4 equal pieces and shape as desired. The depth of your burger will alter the cooking time!
5. Spray the frying pan with low calorie cooking spray and place the burgers in to cook. Don't turn the heat too high or the outside will burn before the burgers are cooked.
6. Turn the burgers after around 4-5 minutes and cook for a further 4-5 minutes on the second side. Don't try to turn the burgers too soon or they may fall apart. The burgers should be well browned and cooked through without having dried out. Serve with your choice of accompaniment!

Chicken Kievs

PREP TIME 10 COOK TIME 30 SERVINGS 4

Ingredients

- 4 chicken breast skin and visible fat removed
- 60 g wholemeal bread
- 2 eggs
- 20 g reduced fat spread
- 1 handful fresh parsley
- 3 garlic cloves
- 2 vegetable stock pots
- 2 tsp water
- sea salt
- freshly ground pepper

Instructions

1. Pre-heat the oven to 170°C and line a baking tray with greaseproof paper.
2. Into a mini electric chopper place the garlic, parsley, vegetable stock pots, water and reduced fat spread. Whizz until the garlic and parsley are chopped, being careful not to form a paste. Place into a dish and chill for 15 minutes.
3. Using the mini electric chopper, whizz the bread into fine breadcrumbs.
4. Using a very sharp knife, cut a pocket into the chicken – place the knife into one end, being careful not to cut through to the outside.
5. Once the garlic mixture has chilled, spoon evenly into the pocket in the chicken breasts, filling as much as possible. Pin closed with a cocktail stick.
6. Beat the eggs and place into a shallow dish. Place the breadcrumbs into a separate shallow dish. Dip each chicken breast into the egg, and then lightly cover with breadcrumbs in the second dish.
7. Place each crumbed chicken breast onto the baking tray, spray with low calorie cooking spray and cook for 30 minutes until golden and crisp. Serve with a wedge of lemon and your choice of accompaniment!

Crispy Chilli Beef

PREP TIME 10 **COOK TIME** 25 **SERVINGS** 4

Ingredients

- 500 g lean rump steak cut into thin strips
- 1 egg beaten
- 1.5 tbsp self raising flour
- 6 tbsp soy sauce, preferably dark
- 2 cloves garlic finely chopped
- 1.5 cm piece ginger peeled and finely chopped
- 3 tbsp rice vinegar
- 1 red pepper deseeded and sliced
- 1/2 onion sliced
- 5 spring onions chopped
- 1 lime juice only
- 1 carrot cut into thin strips
- 2 good pinches chilli flakes or 1/2 chopped red chilli
- 2 drops Franks Buffalo Wings Hot Sauce or another hot/chilli sauce
- 2 tsp granulated sweetener
- 1 tsp honey
- 1/2 Oxo cube made up with 100ml boiling water
- low calorie cooking spray
- sea salt
- freshly ground black pepper

Instructions

1. Pre-heat the oven to 190-200°C.
2. Season the strips of beef, then dip each one into the beaten egg, then quickly drag it through the flour to give a light coating.
3. Place each piece of coated beef on a baking tray sprayed with a fair bit of low calorie cooking spray, then give the strips a spray too. You could even put it on a piece of baking parchment to ensure it doesn't stick.
4. Cook for 20-25 minutes, until the beef is crispy. You can turn it over towards the end if needed.
5. While the beef is cooking, spray a wok with some low calorie cooking spray. Then over a medium/hot heat, fry the peppers, carrots, onion, spring onion, chilli flakes, garlic and ginger.
6. Cook for 5 minutes, then add the lime juice, granulated sweetener, soy sauce, rice vinegar and honey.
7. Stir, then add a couple of drops of Franks sauce and the 100ml of beef stock.
8. Allow to cook for a minute and then add the cooked beef strips.
9. Stir well and serve with your choice of accompaniment.

Diet Coke / Pepsi Max Chicken

PREP TIME 10　　**COOK TIME** 25　　**SERVINGS** 4

Ingredients

- 2 chicken breasts diced
- 1/2 tsp Chinese 5 spice
- sea salt
- 1 red onion sliced
- 6 mushrooms quartered
- 3 cloves garlic finely chopped
- 1.5 cm fresh ginger finely chopped
- 2 tbsp tomato puree
- 1 tbsp Worcestershire sauce
- 2 tbsp dark soy sauce
- 1 tbsp sherry vinegar or you can use balsamic, white wine, red wine or rice vinegar, just not standard vinegar.
- 1/2 red pepper cut into strips
- 1/2 green pepper cut into strips
- 1/2 yellow pepper cut into strips
- 6 baby corn cut in half lengthways
- 1 chicken stock pot
- 1/2 chicken stock cubes
- 1 can Diet Coke or Pepsi Max
- 5 spring onions roughly chopped
- low calorie cooking spray

Instructions

1. Spray a frying pan with low calorie cooking spray and heat gently
2. Add the chicken, sprinkle with the 5 spice and season. Stir and cook until the chicken has started to brown
3. Remove the chicken from the pan, add a few more sprays of low calorie cooking spray then fry off the onions, ginger, garlic and mushrooms
4. Cook until they start to soften
5. Add peppers, baby corn, tomato puree, soy sauce, Worcestershire sauce and vinegar. Stir then add the Coke/Pepsi. Stir and bring to the boil.
6. Stir in the half a stock cube and the stock pot and simmer, uncovered, for 10 minutes
7. When the sauce has started to thicken and go a bit syrupy, return the chicken to the pan and stir in the spring onions
8. Simmer for another 10 minutes. Check the consistency and if it's not quite thick enough simmer for a bit longer, until the required consistency is reached

Chicken Goujons

PREP TIME 20   **COOK TIME** 40   **SERVINGS** 4

Ingredients

- 4 Chicken Breasts cut into strips
- 120 g Wholemeal Bread or gluten free roll
- 2 medium Eggs
- 3 tsp Garlic Granules
- 1 Lemon
- 1/2 tsp Freshly Ground Black Pepper
- Sea Salt
- 1/4 tsp Mustard Powder
- 1 small handful Fresh Parsley
- Low Calorie Cooking Spray

Instructions

1. Pre-heat oven to 180°C, line 2 large baking sheets with greaseproof paper and lightly spray with Frylight.
2. Break the bread into pieces and place into a mini chopper, along with the parsley, garlic, salt, pepper, mustard powder and the finely grated rind of the lemon.
3. Beat the eggs and place into a shallow dish. Place the breadcrumb mix into a separate dish.
4. Cut each chicken breast into strips (they should be around 1.5cm thick each). Dip each piece into the egg and then pop into the breadcrumb mix to lightly coat.
5. Once coated, place each piece onto the baking tray. Squeeze over the juice of the lemon.
6. Spray the chicken with low calorie cooking spray and place into the oven for around 25 minutes until golden brown and cooked through.

Katsu Chicken Curry

PREP TIME 10 **COOK TIME** 45 **SERVINGS** 4

Ingredients

- 4 chicken breasts skinless (approximately 150g each)
- 50 g salted tortilla chips crushed
- 1 egg
- 400 g carrot
- 250 g onion
- 230 g potato
- 4 garlic cloves
- 2 chicken stock cubes
- 2 tbsp sweetener
- 2 tbsp soy sauce
- 2 tbsp curry powder We used medium but mild or hot will work too!
- 2 tbsp garlic granules
- 1 tbsp onion granules
- 1 tbsp garam masala
- 750 ml water
- low calorie cooking spray

Instructions

1. Pre-heat the oven to 200°C and chop the garlic, onion, carrots and potato.
2. Spray the pan with low calorie cooking spray and gently fry the onions and garlic for a few minutes.
3. Add the carrots, potato, garlic granules, onion granules, stock cubes, garam masala, curry powder, soy sauce, and the water to the pan and bring to the boil. Then reduce the heat to simmer and put a lid on the pan. It will need to simmer for around 45 minutes, make sure to stir occasionally and add more water if it reduces too much.
4. While the sauce is simmering crush the tortilla chips into crumbs. An easy way to do this is putting them into a sandwich bag and bashing with a rolling pin!
5. Take a baking tray, line with foil and spray with low calorie cooking spray ready for the chicken.
6. Take the egg and whisk it up with a fork in a bowl. Now dip a chicken breast in the egg and lay it on the baking tray. Take a quarter of the crushed tortilla chips and pat onto the top of the chicken. Repeat until all four breasts are coated.
7. Spray the top of the chicken with low calorie cooking spray and place into the middle of the preheated oven. The chicken will take 30-40 minutes to cook depending how thick the breasts are.
8. Once the potato and carrot for the sauce have cooked through, add the sweetener and use a hand blender to liquify the contents of the saucepan. A top tip is to blend twice as long as you think, you want the sauce to be super smooth! If the sauce seems too thick at this point, add some more water a little at a time until you reach the consistency you want. If it seems a little thin, reduce it on a low heat. This is all down to personal preference so don't worry about getting it wrong!
9. When the chicken is done (if you're not sure, make a deep cut in the thickest part of the chicken and check it is white all the way through) slice it up and serve with the sauce!

Dessert & Treats

Millionaire's Shortbread

PREP TIME 30 **COOK TIME** 30 **SERVINGS** 10

Ingredients

For the shortbread layer
- 100 g softened unsalted butter, plus a little extra for greasing
- 25 g caster sugar
- 25 g granulated sweetener
- 150 g plain flour, sifted

For the caramel
- 160 g sugar-free creamy toffees
- 2 tsp light double cream alternative

For the top
- 50 g milk chocolate, broken into pieces

Instructions

1. Preheat the oven to 160°C and grease the cake tin with a little butter, then line the base and sides with non-stick baking paper.
2. Put the butter, sugar and sweetener in a medium bowl and beat with an electric hand whisk or wooden spoon until light and fluffy. Add the flour and stir until combined. Squeeze the mixture together with clean hands to make a smooth ball – you may need damp hands to help bring the dough together (avoid over-handling as this may make the dough tough).
3. Place the dough in the base of the tin and use your knuckles and fingertips to gently press it into a thin, even layer that covers the base. Prick it all over with a fork and bake for 20-25 minutes until light golden. Remove from the oven and leave in the tin to cool completely.
4. For the caramel, put the toffees in a small saucepan over a very low heat and stir for about 2 minutes until just melted. Remove from the heat and stir until completely melted. Stir in the cream alternative. Quickly pour the caramel over the shortbread and spread it out evenly with the back of a spoon. Leave to set for about 20 minutes or until firm.
5. Use the baking paper to transfer the caramel shortbread from the tin to a surface. Melt the chocolate in a small heatproof bowl over a small pan of simmering water, stirring until melted, then drizzle it over the caramel and leave to set. Use a large, sharp knife to cut the shortbread into twenty pieces, remove from the paper and serve.

Chocolate Orange Trifles

PREP TIME 25 **COOK TIME** 10 **SERVINGS** 4

Ingredients

- 4 Jaffa Cakes cut into quarters
- 298 g tinned mandarin oranges in juice, drained
- 11.5 g sachet of sugar free orange jelly crystals
- 285 ml boiling water
- 285 ml cold water

Instructions

1. Place a quartered Jaffa Cake in the base of each glass serving dish.
2. To make the jelly: place the jelly crystals in a heatproof jug. Add the boiling water and stir until dissolved.
3. Add the cold water to the jelly in the jug and stir. Set aside and leave to cool.
4. Divide the drained mandarin oranges between the dishes, placing them on top of the Jaffa Cakes.
5. Pour the cooled jelly over the mandarin oranges and place in the fridge to set for a minimum of 2 hours.
6. To make the custard: place the egg yolk, cornflour, cocoa powder, sweetener and 1 tbsp of the milk in a heatproof jug. Mix until smooth.
7. Place the remaining milk in a small saucepan and place over a medium heat. Heat until steaming hot, taking care not to let the milk burn or boil over.
8. Pour the steaming hot milk into the jug containing the cocoa mixture and stir well.
9. Pour back into the saucepan and return to a medium heat. Stir constantly with a wooden spoon or balloon whisk and cook gently for about 5 minutes, until small bubbles appear on the surface and the custard thickens. As soon as the custard has thickened, remove it from the heat. Don't overheat or boil the custard, as it may split or burn.
10. Scrape the custard into a small bowl to cool. Cover the surface of the custard with cling film to stop a skin forming.

11 When the custard is just cool, remove the cling film and stir with a balloon whisk to ensure it's smooth.
12. Divide the custard between the dishes and spread out to make a thin layer.
13. Place in the fridge and chill for about 30 minutes.
14. When ready to serve, top with a swirl of aerosol cream and drizzle with a little Choc Shot Orange Spice liquid syrup. Place a small Chocolate orange segment on top to decorate. Serve at once.

Biscoff Cheesecake

PREP TIME 15   **COOK TIME** 1HR   **SERVINGS** 10

Ingredients

For the cheesecake
- 175 g Lotus Biscoff biscuits crushed
- 50 g melted reduced fat spread plus a little extra for greasing
- 400 g reduced fat cream cheese
- 400 g 0% fat Greek yoghurt
- 1 tbsp white granulated sweetener
- 2 tbsp Lotus Biscoff spread
- 2 tbsp cornflour
- 2 medium eggs

For the top
- 1 tbsp Lotus Biscoff Spread
- 2 Lotus Biscoff biscuits crushed

Instructions

1. Pre-heat the oven to 140°C.
2. Grease a 20cm tin with a little of the extra reduced fat spread and line the base with some greaseproof paper.
3. Add the crushed biscuits to a bowl and stir in the melted reduced fat spread. Press into the base of the tin. Pop into the fridge whilst you make the cheesecake.
4. Beat together the cream cheese, Greek yoghurt, sweetener, Biscoff spread, cornflour and eggs.
5. Pour the mixture onto the biscuit base and place the tin onto a baking tray.
6. Place on a low shelf in the oven and bake for 50-60 minutes until it's set around the edges but still has a wobble in the centre.
7. Remove from the oven and leave to cool for 1 hour. Once cooled, place in the fridge to chill for a minimum of 2 hours.
8. Remove the cheesecake from the tin and peel away the greaseproof paper, place onto your serving plate.
9. Add the Biscoff spread to a small bowl and microwave for 30 seconds until melted and liquid.
10. Drizzle over the cheesecake and sprinkle over the crumbled Biscoff biscuits. Slice into 10 and serve.

Raspberry & Blueberry Baked Cheesecake

PREP TIME 20   **COOK TIME** 1HR   **SERVINGS** 8

Ingredients

- 400 g 3% fat cream cheese
- 400 g 0% fat Greek yoghurt
- 30 g granulated sweetener
- 1 tsp vanilla extract
- 2 large lemons zested
- 2 tbsp cornflour
- 2 eggs beaten
- 175 g reduced fat digestive biscuits
- 50 g reduced fat spread melted
- 1 tbsp clear honey
- 1/4 tsp ground cinnamon
- low calorie cooking spray

For the topping
- 100 g raspberries
- 100 g blueberries
- 1 tsp clear honey
- 1/4 tsp icing sugar
- handful of mint sprigs

Instructions

1. Pre-heat the oven to 140°c.
2. Grease an 18cm springform tin with low cooking calorie spray. Line the base with a disc of greaseproof paper.
3. Crush the biscuits and stir in the melted reduced fat spread, 1 tbsp honey, cinnamon and the zest of 1 lemon. Press into the base of the springform tin.
4. Using a wooden spoon, beat together the cream cheese, Greek yoghurt, sweetener, vanilla extract, the remaining zest of 1 lemon, cornflour and eggs.
5. Pour the mixture onto the biscuit base and place on a baking tray.
6. Place on a low shelf in the oven and bake for 50 - 60 minutes until it's set around the edges but still wobbly in the centre.
7. Remove from the oven and leave to cool on the baking tray for 1 1/2 hours.
8. Place in the fridge to chill for a minimum of 2 hours.
9. Carefully run a knife around the top edge of the cheesecake to loosen it. Slowly release the clip on the springform tin and then remove the cheesecake.
10. Using a fish slice, lift the cheesecake off the base of the tin and the greaseproof paper. Place on a serving plate.
11. Spread 1 tsp honey over the top of the cheesecake and place the raspberries and blueberries on top. Dust with the icing sugar and decorate with mint sprigs.

Chocolate Lava Mug Cakes

PREP TIME 5 **COOK TIME** 4 **SERVINGS** 4

Ingredients

- 45 g self raising flour
- 25 g granulated sweetener
- 15 g cocoa powder
- 2 medium eggs
- 45 g reduced fat spread
- 1 tsp vanilla extract
- 20 g milk chocolate (4 squares)
- 12 fresh raspberries

Instructions

To cook in the microwave

1. Place all of the ingredients into a mixing bowl (except the chocolate pieces and raspberries) and mix thoroughly until all of the reduced fat spread has been fully mixed into the cake batter.
2. Pour into 4 microwaveable cups or ramekins and pop one square of chocolate onto the top of each.
3. Place into a microwave, one at a time, and cook on high for 1 minute. The cake should be risen but feel light to the touch – if the top is not cooked, place back in the microwave for 30 seconds.
4. Leave to stand for 1 minutes (or while you cook the other cakes!), top with the raspberries and serve!

To cook in the oven

1. Preheat the oven to 160°C.
2. Place all of the ingredients into a mixing bowl (except the chocolate pieces and raspberries) and mix thoroughly until all of the reduced fat spread has been fully mixed into the cake batter.
3. Divide the mixture between 4, ovenproof 125ml ramekins and place a chocolate square on top of each.
4. Place the ramekins onto a baking tray and then pop into the oven for 8 minutes until risen and spongy when pressed, but gooey in middle.
5. Remove from the oven and leave to stand for 5 minutes. Decorate with a raspberry on top of each.

Chocolate Mud Pie

PREP TIME 20　　**COOK TIME** 35　　**SERVINGS** 10

Ingredients

- For the cheesecake
- 120 grams Philadelpia Lightest
- 500 grams quark
- 7 tbsp granulated sweetener
- 2 tbsp cornflour
- 25 grams cocoa powder
- 3 large eggs
- 2 tsp chocolate extract
- 2 tsp coffee granules
- 50 ml boiling water
- For the topping
- 8 grams dark chocolate
- 1 tsp golden caster sugar
- 20 grams oats
- 2 tsp Choc Shot

Instructions

For the mud pie

1. Pre-heat the oven to 200°C, and line an 8inch, loose bottomed cake tin with baking parchment.
2. In a large bowl, mix together the quark, Philadelphia, eggs, granulated sweetener and chocolate extract. Add the coffee granules to the boiling water and add to the mixture. Sift in the cornflour and cocoa powder and stir well to ensure it is thoroughly mixed.
3. Pour the mixture into the lined cake tin and bake for 10 minutes in a hot oven. Turn the oven down after this time to 140°C and bake for a further 25 minutes. Check the mud pie after this - it should have a slight wobble with no runniness.
4. Leave to cool completely and refrigerate for an hour before adding the topping.

For the topping

1. In a dry frying pan, add the caster sugar and oats. It is important to use sugar and no sweetener for this. Leave on a moderate heat, moving the pan occasionally until the sugar has melted and oats have toasted. Leave to cool.
2. Once the mud pie has been refrigerated, take the Choc Shot and spread gently around the edge of the top of the cheese cake. Crush up the caramelised toasted oats as you sprinkle them around the edge and pat gently so they stick to the choc shot.
3. Using a fine grater, grate over the dark chocolate into the centre of the cheesecake. Carefully remove from the tin and slice into 10 pieces and serve.

Banana Bread with Chocolate Chips

PREP TIME 10 **COOK TIME** 40 **SERVINGS** 12

Ingredients

- 56 g self raising four
- 4 eggs
- 1 tsp vanilla extract or essence
- 1 tsp baking powder
- 2 bananas
- 2 tbsp granulated sweetener
- 25 g dark chocolate chips
- low calorie cooking spray

Instructions

1. Sift the flour and baking powder in one bowl.
2. Add the essence, granulated sweetener and mashed bananas.
3. Add 2 of the eggs and mix well.
4. Separate the other 2 eggs and add the yolks to the mixture mixing again.
5. Whisk the 2 whites until very stiff and gently fold into the mixture.
6. Pour into a lined silicone loaf tin (2lb) sprayed with low calorie cooking spray and sprinkle the chocolate chips evenly over the top.
7. Cook in a preheated oven at 180°C for 40 minutes.

Mince Pies

PREP TIME 5 **COOK TIME** 22 **SERVINGS** 12

Ingredients

- 3 Weight Watchers Wraps
- 12 tsp mincemeat
- 1 egg

Instructions

1. Preheat the oven to 180°C.
2. Using a circular pastry cutter, cut 12 circles, just larger than each dip of the muffin tin. Also cut 12 small star shapes – you should have enough space in 3 wraps to cut all the items you need.
3. Push each circle of wrap carefully into each dip in the muffin tin. Place a teaspoon of mincemeat into each one and top with a small star.
4. Beat the egg in a small bowl and brush over each star. Place into the oven for 22 minutes until golden and crisp.

Apple Strudels

PREP TIME 10 **COOK TIME** 10 **SERVINGS** 1

Ingredients

- 2 eggs yolk and white separated
- 1 tsp granulated sweetener
- 5 strawberries (around 65g) stalks removed and sliced
- 1 tsp reduced sugar strawberry jam
- 1/8 tsp icing sugar for dusting
- low calorie cooking spray

Instructions

1. Place the apple in a microwavable bowl, and stir in the cinnamon, sweetener and water. Cover with cling film and cook on high for a couple of minutes or until it starts to soften, but still has a bit of a bite.
2. Remove the apple, drain off any excess water and measure out 60g (half a cup) of cooked apple (save the rest for another day!).
3. Mix the mincemeat with the apple and set aside.
4. Take the wrap and fold it into 3 equal sections. Press firmly so you can see the marks when you unfold it.
5. Open out the wrap and fold it in half. When you do this you should be able to see the marks you made earlier.
6. Using a sharp knife make a cut from the line to the edge of the wrap.
7. Measure a fingers width and make another cut at the same angle. Continue cutting, you should get around 7-9 strips, leaving the top and bottom of the wrap uncut.
8. Brush the whole wrap with beaten egg, paying extra attention to the edges so they stick.
9. Spoon the apple and mincemeat along the middle of the wrap.
10. Fold the bottom of the wrap in, then starting at the end closest to you fold the bottom left strip up towards the top right hand corner of the wrap.
11. Fold the bottom right strip over towards the top left corner of the wrap.
12. Once you are halfway up, fold in the top flap. Continue alternating the remaining strips until all the filling is enclosed.
13. Place on a baking try that has been sprayed with low calorie cooking spray and brush the remaining egg wash on the surface of the strudel bake for 10 minutes at 200°C or until they are golden brown.

Strawberry Souffle Omelette

PREP TIME 10 **COOK TIME** 5 **SERVINGS** 1

Ingredients

- 2 eggs yolk and white separated
- 1 tsp granulated sweetener
- 5 strawberries (around 65g) stalks removed and sliced
- 1 tsp reduced sugar strawberry jam
- 1/8 tsp icing sugar for dusting
- low calorie cooking spray

Instructions

1. Spray an ovenproof frying pan with low calorie cooking spray and grease thoroughly. Mix the strawberries with the jam and set aside.
2. Place the egg yolks and sweetener in a large bowl and beat with an electric whisk for 1 - 2 minutes, until well combined. The mixture will still be runny at this stage.
3. Wash the whisks in hot soapy water and dry thoroughly before proceeding.
4. Place the egg whites in a mixing bowl and whisk until stiff peaks have formed.
5. Tip the whisked egg whites into the egg yolk mixture and, using a large metal spoon, fold in until just combined. Take care not to knock the air out of the mixture.
6. Place the greased frying pan on a medium heat. When hot, tip in the egg mixture and gently spread out to a diameter of approximately 15cm. Preheat the grill on a medium setting.
7. Cook the omelette in the frying pan for 2 - 3 minutes, or until the edges start to dry. Carefully lift the edge to look underneath, the base should be light golden.
8. Place the omelette in the frying pan under the preheated grill, and grill for 1 - 2 minutes until the top is light golden brown.
9. Transfer the omelette to a serving plate.
10. Place the strawberry mixture on one half of the omelette and fold the other half over the top. Dust with the icing sugar and serve at once.

Peach and Blueberry Tart

PREP TIME 5   **COOK TIME** 20   **SERVINGS** 8

Ingredients

- 320 g sheet light puff pastry
- 2 medium peaches, stone removed and thinly sliced
- 60 g blueberries
- 3 tbsp extra light cream cheese
- 1 tbsp reduced sugar apricot jam
- 1 tsp skimmed milk

Instructions

1. Preheat the oven to 190°C and line a baking tray with greaseproof paper.
2. Add the cream cheese and jam to a small bowl and mix to combine.
3. Lay the puff pastry out on the lined baking tray and use a sharp knife to score a 1cm border around the edge of the pastry.
4. Spread the cream cheese mixture onto the puff pastry, all the way up to the edge of the scored border.
5. Add your sliced peaches and dot the blueberries in any of the gaps.
6. Brush the border of the pastry with the skimmed milk and pop into the oven for 20 minutes, until the pastry border is golden brown and the peaches are just starting to colour.
7. Slice into 8 portions and serve with ice cream, custard or yoghurt!

Lemon Tiramisu

PREP TIME 152 **COOK TIME** 10 **SERVINGS** 4

Ingredients

- For the lemon syrup:
- 1 lemon peel removed, cut into wide strips with the juice squeezed
- 100 ml cold water
- 1 tbsp white granulated sweetener or caster sugar
- For the filling:
- 250 g ricotta
- 4 tbsp lemon curd
- 8 sponge fingers halved
- 4 tsp lemon curd
- For the top:
- 4 tsp lemon curd to decorate
- 2 halved lemon slices to decorate

Instructions

1. Remove all the white pith from the lemon peel using a small sharp knife. If the white pith remains it will make the syrup bitter. Place the peel in a small saucepan and add the water. Place on a low heat and gently simmer for 10 minutes to infuse the flavour and colour of the lemon peel.
2. Remove from the heat, strain the syrup into a bowl and discard the lemon peel. Add the sweetener or sugar and stir until dissolved. Stir in the lemon juice and leave to cool for 5 minutes. Set aside.
3. For the filling: Put the ricotta and 4 tbsp of lemon curd in a small mixing bowl and beat together with a wooden spoon until smooth. Set aside.
4. Dip the sponge finger halves in the lemon syrup, allowing them to soak up the syrup but not to become mushy. Place two sponge finger halves in the bottom of each dish.
5. Divide half of the filling between the four dishes and roughly spread over the sponge fingers. Add a teaspoonful of lemon curd to each dish and roughly swirl into the filling.
6. Place another two sponge finger halves in each dish and top with the remaining creamy lemon filling. Roughly spread over the sponge fingers and add a teaspoonful of lemon curd to the top of each tiramisu, swirling it roughly on top. Chill for 2 hours and decorate each tiramisu with half a lemon slice.

Crustless Apple Pie

PREP TIME 10 **COOK TIME** 30 **SERVINGS** 6

Ingredients

- 6 cooking apples, peeled and sliced
- 80 g self raising flour
- 45 g granulated sweetener
- 100 g 0% fat Greek yoghurt
- 100 ml skimmed milk
- 2 eggs, beaten
- 1 tsp cinnamon
- low-calorie cooking spray

Instructions

1. Preheat the oven to 180°C.
2. Combine the beaten egg, Greek yoghurt and milk in a mixing bowl and whisk together.
3. Add in the flour, sweetener and cinnamon, and whisk until you have a smooth batter.
4. Once the batter is smooth, add the sliced apples and mix until they're coated.
5. Spray the oven or pie dish with some low-calorie cooking spray and pour in the apple batter mixture.
6. Pop in the oven for 30 minutes, until the top is lightly golden and the pie is firm and set.
7. Leave to cool for 5 minutes, then slice and serve with your choice of accompaniment. We love it with a scoop of low-calorie vanilla ice cream.

Chocolate and Orange Cake

PREP TIME 10   **COOK TIME** 30   **SERVINGS** 8

Ingredients

- 50 g self raising flour
- 3 tbsp granulated sweetener
- 25 g cocoa powder
- 1 large orange
- 5 eggs

Instructions

1. Remove the zest from the orange using a hand grater and separate the egg whites from the yolks.
2. Mix together the flour, cocoa powder, sweetener (reserve 1 teaspoon for the drizzle) the orange zest, juice of 1/2 the orange and 5 egg yolks. If this mixture is a bit dry then you can add a little water to make it easier to mix in the whisked egg whites.
3. In another bowl whisk the egg whites until they form soft peaks.
4. Gently fold the egg whites into the flour and egg yolk mixture, until they are mixed evenly.
5. Pour the mixture into a 2lb loaf tin (we lined the bottom with baking parchment and gave it a quick spray with low calorie cooking spray just in case).
6. Bake for 25-30 minutes at 180°C until golden brown or until the knife comes out clean. Don't be tempted to check it before 25 minutes or the cake will sink!
7. While the cake is cooking, mix the remaining sweetener with the rest of the orange juice and heat on low in a sauce pan.
8. When the cake is done (to check insert a knife and it should come out clean) remove it from the oven, turn the heat down to 100°C then pour the orange syrup over the top of the cake and put it back in for another 10 minutes.
9. Leave to cool, and then cut into 8 equal slices.

Chocolate Brownie Trifle

PREP TIME 25
COOK TIME 12
SERVINGS 4

Ingredients

- For the brownies
- 50 g self raising flour
- 25 g reduced fat spread
- 2 eggs
- 2 tbsp white granulated sweetener
- 1 tbsp cocoa powder
- 2 tsp low-calorie chocolate syrup
- ½ tsp baking powder
- 10 g chocolate chips
- For the jelly layer
- 11½ g sachet of raspberry sugar free jelly crystals
- 100 ml boiling water
- 100 ml cold water
- 50 g raspberries
- To assemble
- 100 g 0% Greek yoghurt
- 100 g light custard
- 100 g raspberries, leave 8 raspberries whole but slice the rest in half
- low fat aerosol cream
- 20 g chocolate flake bar, crumbled

Instructions

1. Add the jelly crystals to a measuring jug and pour in the boiling water. Stir until the crystals have dissolved, then add the cold water and stir again. Split between the 4 serving dishes and add the raspberries. Pop in the fridge until the jelly is set.
2. Preheat the oven to 170°C. Grease 4 holes in the silicone muffin tin with a little reduced fat spread.
3. Place the reduced fat spread, granulated sweetener, baking powder, self raising flour, eggs, cocoa and chocolate syrup into a large mixing bowl and mix thoroughly.
4. Pour into the silicone muffin tin and sprinkle over the chocolate chips. Place in the oven for 12 minutes. Leave to one side to cool.
5. Mix the Greek yoghurt and custard together in a small mixing bowl until just combined. You should still be able to see the Greek yoghurt swirled into the custard. Once the brownies are cooled, cut each one into 6 pieces.
6. Once the jelly is set, you're ready to assemble. Spoon some of the custard mixture on top of the jelly layer and top with 3 pieces of brownie and the halved raspberries. Top with the rest of the custard mixture.
7. Add a swirl of aerosol cream to the top of each trifle then add the remaining brownie pieces, whole raspberries and sprinkle over the crumbled flake.

Biscoff Lava Cakes

PREP TIME 10 **COOK TIME** 2 **SERVINGS** 4

Ingredients

- 45 g self raising flour
- 25 g white granulated sweetener
- 60 g smooth Biscoff spread
- 45 g reduced fat spread
- 2 medium eggs
- 1 tsp caramel flavouring
- 4 tsp smooth Biscoff spread, for the centre
- ¼ tsp icing sugar, for dusting
- a little extra reduced fat spread, for greasing

Instructions

1. Grease 4 x 125ml ramekin dishes with a little extra reduced fat spread.
2. Place the self raising flour, sweetener, Biscoff spread, reduced fat spread, eggs and caramel flavouring in a medium mixing bowl. Beat together for 1-2 minutes using an electric whisk or wooden spoon until smooth and creamy.
3. Divide the mixture between the 4 ramekin dishes. Drop a teaspoonful of Biscoff spread into the centre of each.
4. Place all 4 ramekins on the microwave turntable, evenly spaced apart. Cover loosely with cling film and cook on high for 1 1/2 - 2 minutes. Check on the cakes after about a minute and continue cooking if needed. The cakes will be ready when they're risen and spongy but still runny in the centre. Leave to stand for 5 minutes, then remove the cling film.
5. Dust with a little icing sugar and serve at once. Serve alone, or with a swirl of reduced fat aerosol cream or a little custard.

Banoffee Tiramisu

PREP TIME 15

SERVINGS 4

Ingredients

- 2 medium bananas peeled and thinly slices
- 2 tsp lemon juice
- 300 g ricotta cheese
- 2 tsp vanilla extract
- 3 tbsp white granulated sweetener
- 8 sponge fingers halved
- 1 tbsp instant coffee granules
- 6 tbsp boiling water
- 8 tsp reduced sugar chocolate dessert topping
- 8 tsp reduced sugar caramel dessert topping
- To decorate:
- 2 tsp reduced sugar caramel dessert topping
- ¼ tsp cocoa powder

Instructions

1. Mix the instant coffee with 6 tbsp of boiling water and stir until dissolved. Leave to cool.
2. Place the bananas on a plate and sprinkle with the lemon juice. Turn the banana slices over until coated with the lemon juice. This will stop the bananas from turning brown. Set aside.
3. Place the ricotta, vanilla extract and white granulated sweetener in a medium mixing bowl. Stir with a wooden spoon until smooth and set aside.
4. Place two sponge finger halves in the bottom of each serving dish. Divide 3 tbsp of the dissolved coffee between the four dishes, drizzling it over the sponge fingers.
5. Drizzle 1 tsp of chocolate dessert topping and 1 tsp of caramel dessert topping over the sponge fingers in each dish.
6. Place a dessert spoonful of the ricotta mixture on top of the sponge fingers in each dish and spread over.
7. Reserve 8 banana slices for decoration then divide the rest of the bananas between the four dishes, spreading out evenly.
8. Place two sponge finger halves on top of the ricotta in each dish and drizzle with the remaining 3 tbsp of dissolved coffee.
9. Drizzle each with 1 tsp of chocolate dessert topping and 1 tsp of caramel dessert topping.
10. Divide the remaining ricotta mixture between the four dishes and roughly smooth over the top.
11. Cover with cling film and place in the fridge for a minimum of 2 hours to allow the sponge fingers to absorb the coffee and for the flavours to mingle.
12. Just before serving, drizzle the top of each with 1/2 tsp of caramel sauce and dust with a little cocoa powder. Place two of the reserved banana slices on top and serve.

Banana Cream Pudding

PREP TIME 10   **COOK TIME** 10   **SERVINGS** 4

Ingredients

- 250 ml semi-skimmed milk
- 2 bananas
- 2 egg yolks
- 150 ml Elmlea Double Light
- 1 tbsp cornflour
- 1 tbsp granulated sweetener or sugar
- 1 treat size Flake
- a few drops of vanilla essence

Instructions

1. Firstly, make your custard.
2. Heat the milk in a saucepan until it is hot but not boiling.
3. In a mixing bowl, whisk together the egg yolks, cornflour, sweetener or sugar and vanilla essence.
4. When the milk is hot, whisk it into the egg mixture a little at a time. Be careful to add it slowly. If you pour it in too fast you will scramble the eggs!
5. Pour the custard mix back into the pan, and place on a low heat. Keep whisking until it thickens and bubbles begin to break the surface. Don't be tempted to rush this. Increasing the heat will curdle the sauce and you will end up with a scrambled eggy mess! Allow the bubbles to break the surface for 30 seconds while you continue to whisk, then take off the heat.
6. Scrape out of the pan into a bowl cover with cling film and allow to cool. When cold enough, pop it into the fridge for half an hour to chill.
7. When cold, finely chop or lightly mash the bananas reserving a few slices for decoration and stir them into the cold custard.
8. Whip the cream until thick and fold into the banana custard mix.
9. Spoon into 4 individual glass dishes, top with the crumbled Flake and reserved banana slices. Enjoy!

Butterscotch Tarts

PREP TIME 15   **COOK TIME** 15   **SERVINGS** 12

Ingredients

- 3 low calorie tortilla wraps
- 50 g reduced fat spread
- 25 g soft light brown sugar
- 25 g brown granulated sweetener
- 50 ml semi skimmed milk
- 1 tbsp cornflour
- a few drops of vanilla essence
- a few drops of butterscotch flavouring

Instructions

1. Preheat the oven to 160°C.
2. To make the tart cases: cut out 12 x 8cm rounds from the tortilla wraps using a plain round 8 cm cutter. If you don't have a cutter, you can use a round 8cm glass and cut around it using a small sharp knife.
3. Use the rounds to line the bun tin, pressing into each hole. Place a small square of greaseproof paper on top of each round then pour in the ceramic baking beans in each tart case to hold them down whilst baking. If you haven't got ceramic baking beans, you can use something else such as dried beans, uncooked rice or just some scrunched up foil to do the same job.
4. Place the lined bun tray in the preheated oven for about 5 minutes until the tart cases are lightly golden.
5. Remove from the oven and lift out the greaseproof paper and ceramic baking beans. Place the tart cases on a cooling rack and leave to cool.
6. To make the butterscotch filling: place the reduced fat spread, soft light brown sugar, brown granulated sweetener, vanilla essence and butterscotch flavouring in a small saucepan. Place over a low heat and stir for about 5 minutes until just dissolved. Remove from the heat as soon as it has dissolved. Don't let the mixture bubble or boil.
7. Place the cornflour in a small bowl and mix with 1 tbsp of the milk, until smooth.

8 our the remaining milk into the melted reduced fat spread, sugar, sweetener, vanilla essence and butterscotch flavouring and stir. Place back on a medium heat and stir in the cornflour mixture, stirring constantly with a wooden spoon or balloon whisk.

9 Keep stirring and cook gently for about 4 - 5 minutes, until smooth, glossy and thickened. Don't overheat and boil the mixture otherwise it may burn.

10 Place 1 1/2 tsp of the butterscotch filling in each tart case and spread out a little by tilting the cases.

11 Leave to cool and set for about 30 minutes.

12 Serve alone or with an accompaniment of your choice such as custard, or serve with a selection of other tea time biscuits and cakes.

White Chocolate Mousse with Raspberry

PREP TIME 5

SERVINGS 6

Ingredients

- 284 ml 50% less fat double cream alternative
- 22 g white chocolate flavour Options hot chocolate powder
- ½ tsp Dr Oetker Vege-Gel
- 125 g raspberries fresh or frozen
- 2 tsp granulated sweetener
- 2 tbsp water

Instructions

1. Place the cream alternative, white chocolate Options drink powder and Vege-Gel into a large bowl. Whisk using an electric hand whisk until it is thick and has doubled in volume.
2. Carefully spoon the mousse into your chosen container and pop in the fridge for at least 2 hours, or ideally overnight, to set.
3. When ready to serve, turn out from the mould (if using) by dipping into some hot water (careful not to get the mousse wet!) and running a thin knife around the edge.
4. Make the coulis by placing all the remaining ingredients into a food processor and blitzing until blended. Place a bowl underneath a sieve and strain the coulis into it to remove all the seeds - you might need to push the liquid through the sieve with a spoon.
5. Serve the coulis on top of your mousse and enjoy

Rice Pudding

PREP TIME 5 **COOK TIME** 20 **SERVINGS** 4

Ingredients

- 350 g arborio rice or pudding rice
- 800 ml Alpro Coconut Drink (No added sugar)
- 3 tbsp granulated sweetener
- 1 whole lime
- 4 whole passion fruit
- 1 whole vanilla pod

Instructions

1. Add the rice and milk to a saucepan on a low heat. Cut the vanilla pod in two and scoop out the seeds, adding them and the pod to the saucepan. Cook for around 20 minutes, stirring occasionally until the rice is tender and creamy.
2. Once cooked, stir in the sweetener and the juice and zest of the lime.
3. Serve immediately topped with one half of the scooped out passion fruit on top, and one half to garnish.

Eton Mess

PREP TIME 10 **SERVINGS** 4

Ingredients

- 500 grams fat free Greek yoghurt
- 400 grams strawberries
- 8 macaringues, approx 2.5g each
- 1 tsp vanilla extract
- 1 tbsp granulated sweetener
- 1 whole lemon

Instructions

1. Add the yoghurt and granulated sweetener to a large mixing bowl. Chop the strawberries into bite sized pieces and add to the yoghurt. Mix in the vanilla extract and then add the juice and zest of the lemon.
2. Choosing 6 different coloured Macaringues, crush into the yoghurt and fruit mixture and carefully mix – do not over mix as the Macaringes are fragile and will break up easily!
3. Serve immediately in individual dishes – crush the remaining Macaringues on top and garnish with a whole strawberry.

Christmas Trifle

PREP TIME 30   COOK TIME 10   SERVINGS 8

Ingredients

For the fruit and sponge filling
- 20 sponge fingers
- 800 g mixed berries such as blackberries, strawberries, blackcurrants, red currants and raspberries, defrosted and their juices kept
- 2 oranges peeled, all pith removed, cut into round slices and quartered
- 2 nectarines stoned and cut into segments
- 70 g white granulated sweetener
- 2 tsp mixed spice

For the custard
- 500 ml semi skimmed milk
- 3 medium egg yolks
- 2 tsp vanilla extract
- 2 tbsp cornflour
- 50 g white granulated sweetener

For the mascarpone filling
- 250 g reduced fat mascarpone
- 30 g icing sugar
- 2 tbsp semi skimmed milk
- For decoration
- 8 raspberries
- 8 small sprigs of mint
- 10 g flaked almonds toasted

Instructions

For the fruit and sponge filling
1. Place the defrosted mixed berries and their juices in a medium mixing bowl. Add the orange pieces, the nectarine segments, the sweetener and the mixed spice and gently stir.
2. Place 3 sponge fingers in the bottom of the serving bowl. Place a large serving spoonful of the fruit mixture on top of the sponge fingers (this will provide support for the sponge fingers that will stand on their ends around the inside of the bowl).
3. Place 10 upright sponge fingers at equal intervals around the inside of the serving bowl.
4. Place half of the fruit into the serving bowl, gently pushing it into the spaces between the sponge fingers and levelling the fruit mixture.
5. Place the remaining 7 sponge fingers on top of the fruit. Spread the remaining fruit over the sponge fingers and level the top.

For the custard
1. Place the egg yolks, vanilla, cornflour and sweetener in a heatproof measuring jug and stir to form a smooth mixture.
2. Place the milk in a medium saucepan and place over a medium heat, until just steaming hot, taking care not to let it burn or boil over.
3. Pour the hot milk into the mixture in the jug, stir, then immediately pour back into the saucepan and place over a medium heat.
4. Stir the custard mixture constantly with a wooden spoon or balloon whisk, for about 5 minutes until gently bubbling and thickened.
5. Remove from the heat and leave to cool slightly. Stir occasionally whilst cooling to stop a skin forming on top of the custard.

For the custard
1. Place the egg yolks, vanilla, cornflour and sweetener in a heatproof measuring jug and stir to form a smooth mixture.
2. Place the milk in a medium saucepan and place over a medium heat, until just steaming hot, taking care not to let it burn or boil over.
3. Pour the hot milk into the mixture in the jug, stir, then immediately pour back into the saucepan and place over a medium heat.
4. Stir the custard mixture constantly with a wooden spoon or balloon whisk, for about 5 minutes until gently bubbling and thickened.
5. Remove from the heat and leave to cool slightly. Stir occasionally whilst cooling to stop a skin forming on top of the custard.
6. Pour the warm custard over the fruit and sponge then leave to cool.
7. Once cooled, cover with cling film and place in the fridge for about 40 minutes or until the custard has set.

For the topping
1. Place the mascarpone, icing sugar and milk in a small bowl and stir with a wooden spoon until smooth and the consistency of lightly whipped cream.
2. Spread the topping over the top of the trifle, swirling with a small palette knife.
3. Decorate the top of the trifle with fresh raspberries, sprigs of mint and toasted flaked almonds.
4. Cover with cling film and chill for 3 – 4 hours, or overnight.
5. Serve alone or with a squirt of aerosol cream if wished.

Christmas Chocolate Log

PREP TIME 20 **COOK TIME** 14 **SERVINGS** 10

Ingredients

For the sponge
- 4 medium eggs
- 50 g white granulated sweetener
- 50 g caster sugar
- 1 tsp vanilla essence
- 75 g self raising flour
- 25 g cocoa powder
- low calorie cooking spray

For the frosting
- 250 g low fat cream cheese
- 25 g cocoa powder
- 50 g white granulated sweetener
- 4 tbsp water

For the decoration
- 3 raspberries or other edible red berries like redcurrants or cranberries
- 1/4 tsp icing sugar
- sprig of holly

Instructions

1. Pre-heat the oven to 160°C.
2. Spray a 26 x 38 cm Swiss roll tin or shallow baking tray with a little low calorie cooking spray and use to grease the tin.
3. Line the base and sides of the tin with baking parchment paper.

For the sponge

1. Place the eggs, sweetener, caster sugar and vanilla essence in a large bowl. Whisk with a hand held electric whisk for about 10 minutes on high speed, until thick, pale and creamy. The mixture needs to be thick enough for a 'ribbon' trail to be left on the surface when the whisk is lifted out.
2. Sift together the flour and cocoa powder into a medium bowl. Sift once more, into the whisked mixture.
3. Using a large metal spoon, gently fold the flour and cocoa powder in until just evenly mixed. Be careful not to over mix the mixture otherwise you will knock out the air you have incorporated.
4. Pour the mixture into the prepared tin and gently spread out using a palette knife.
5. Place in the oven for 10 - 12 minutes. Gently press the centre of the sponge, if it springs back and leaves no indent then it is ready.
6. Remove from the oven and turn out, sponge side down, onto a sheet of baking parchment paper.
7. Carefully peel away the lining paper from the sponge and discard.

8. Using a round bladed knife, score a line along the narrow end nearest to you, approx 2.5 cm in from the edge.

9. Whilst the sponge is still warm, and starting from the scored narrow end, carefully roll up into a Swiss roll, using the sheet of baking parchment paper to help you. Make sure the Swiss roll is seam side down and leave to cool completely on the sheet of baking paper.

For the frosting

1. Place the cocoa powder, white granulated sweetener and water in a small saucepan and stir with a wooden spoon until smooth. Place over a low heat and bring to a gentle simmer.
2. Simmer gently, for 1 - 2 minutes, stirring, until smooth, glossy and the consistency of melted chocolate. Using a spatula, scrape into a small bowl and leave until just cool.
3. Place the cream cheese in a medium bowl and mix with a wooden spoon until softened and smooth. Add the cocoa mixture and stir until evenly mixed.
4. Carefully unroll the cooled Swiss roll on the baking parchment paper. Spread half of the frosting evenly over the sponge, and roll up to form a Swiss roll. Transfer to a serving plate, and place it seam side down.
5. Spread the remaining frosting all over the Swiss roll, and roughly texture with a small palette knife to resemble bark. Decorate with a sprig of holly, and red berries of your choice. Dust with icing sugar and chill for a minimum of 1 hour before cutting into 10 slices.

Banana Bread Pudding

PREP TIME 5 **COOK TIME** 35 **SERVINGS** 10

Ingredients

- 4 medium eggs
- 50 g self raising flour
- 30 g granulated sweetener
- 2 medium bananas, approx. 200g, mashed well
- 2 tsp mixed spice
- 25 g sultanas

Instructions

1. Preheat the oven to 160°C and line the bottom of a loaf tin.
2. Separate 2 of the eggs into two mixing bowls, yolks in one and whites in the other. To the bowl with the yolks add the flour, 2 eggs, sweetener, banana and mixed spice, mix well until fully combined.
3. Whisk the egg whites with an electric whisk to firm peaks.
4. Fold the egg whites carefully into the banana mixture being careful not to knock out all the air. Stir in the sultanas.
5. Scrape the mixture into the loaf tin and bake for 25-35 minutes until cooked through and turning golden brown.

Printed in Great Britain
by Amazon